Unlocking Business Agility with Evidence-Based Management

T0293260

Unlocking Business Agility with Evidence-Based Management

SATISFY CUSTOMERS AND IMPROVE ORGANIZATIONAL EFFECTIVENESS

Patricia Kong
Todd Miller
Kurt Bittner
Ryan Ripley

Addison-Wesley

Library of Congress Control Number: 2023945379

ISBN-13: 978-0-13-824457-6
ISBN-10: 0-13-824457-X

3 2023

Pearson's Commitment to Diversity, Equity, and Inclusion

Pearson is dedicated to creating bias-free content that reflects the diversity of all learners. We embrace the many dimensions of diversity, including but not limited to race, ethnicity, gender, socioeconomic status, ability, age, sexual orientation, and religious or political beliefs.

Education is a powerful force for equity and change in our world. It has the potential to deliver opportunities that improve lives and enable economic mobility. As we work with authors to create content for every product and service, we acknowledge our responsibility to demonstrate inclusivity and incorporate diverse scholarship so that everyone can achieve their potential through learning. As the world's leading learning company, we have a duty to help drive change and live up to our purpose to help more people create a better life for themselves and to create a better world.

Our ambition is to purposefully contribute to a world where:

- Everyone has an equitable and lifelong opportunity to succeed through learning.
- Our educational products and services are inclusive and represent the rich diversity of learners.
- Our educational content accurately reflects the histories and experiences of the learners we serve.
- Our educational content prompts deeper discussions with learners and motivates them to expand their own learning (and worldview).

While we work hard to present unbiased content, we want to hear from you about any concerns or needs with this Pearson product so that we can investigate and address them.

- Please contact us with concerns about any potential bias at https://www.pearson.com/report-bias.html.

CONTENTS

FOREWORD BY KEN SCHWABER

Evidence is like a critic, pointing out our shortcomings. We are free to disregard or disbelieve it, or we can investigate and see if there is any merit to what it says.

Software product development is complex. The individual components of people, tools, and transformation of ideas to working software and products have more parts that are unknown or argued over than are known and agreed upon. As they are conglomerated, the result needs to be known to power the heart of empiricism: inspect and adapt.

Given that morass, we need to create the product in short iterations, progressively turning the most important ideas, needs, and requirements into valuable increments that build on each other until the vision is achieved—if the vision is even possible.

We use empiricism to continue as long as our efforts create more value than cost.

Empiricism uses frequent inspection of the work in progress to achieve the best outcomes. The work generates regular well-known artifacts. To maximize the value of these adaptations, we must ensure the artifacts are well understood and conform to certain standards ("Done") that are based on frequent decisions of what is happening, are realistic, and do not cling to desire.

SCRUM

We presented Scrum to the world more than 30 years ago. Many teams and organizations have used it to deliver valuable solutions to complex problems. Scrum is a framework within which a team of people can address a complex problem to create an increment of value within a short period of time.

What follows is the problem as we saw it at the time:

> **Problem:** Most software development projects failed to deliver the expected functionality on the committed date for the budgeted cost.
>
> **Cause:** Software development is a complex endeavor that requires a process that relies on the art of the possible, not fantasies of the improbable.
>
> **Solution:** Utilize a process that is not fixed but adapts visions into goals that *are* possible. Flexibility is important. Empiricism was reflected in the growth of iterative, incremental development processes in the 1990s.

In Scrum, a well-understood artifact, the *increment*, is generated and shown by the end of each iteration, or *sprint*. It must be complete and "done," or everyone inspecting it will see things differently and want adaptations that suit narrowly defined needs. Undone work undoes Scrum.

How valuable is Scrum to your organization?

We see from the Standish Group that the success rate of waterfall projects is less than 20 percent. In contrast, Scrum projects achieved a 90 percent success rate by 2015. (You can find details at their websites and in their publications.)

However, closer to home, ask anyone at an organization that uses Scrum how things are going. You might hear, "excellent," "pretty good," "better than before," "awful," or "another fad." Those are interesting responses. Notice that these are only opinions, not facts. These are also not the basis of actions to optimize short-term or long-term value.

As we worked with organizations to adopt Scrum, we realized that their whole organization had similar issues to what software teams using Scrum had. Both teams and organizations found themselves wondering, "What is value, and how do we know if we are delivering it? Is Scrum working for us?"

EVIDENCE-BASED MANAGEMENT

To help them understand this, we studied and adapted the evidence-based medicine that is used in healthcare organizations for software development. We developed metrics that manage product and software development, regardless of the overall process, and created a framework that we call Evidence-Based Management (EBM).

Consistent, known measures facilitate optimal outcomes based on intelligent adaptations, which we have evolved into different Key Value Areas (KVAs). We looked at metrics measuring (broadly) a product's

- Current value, which is a measure of the outcomes that customers experience by using the product
- Time to market, which is a measure of the intervals at which the organization delivers new product increments
- Ability to innovate, or measures of the effectiveness of the organization in delivering valuable increments

Over time, we saw a need for a fourth kind of measure that we called unrealized value, which looked at the potential value that the organization might deliver but currently does not deliver.

Although the KVAs gave organizations a way to measure both the value they delivered and their ability to deliver it, they also needed a reason to deliver value. They needed goals and a way to align their value delivery with their broader organizational goals—not just strategic goals, but shorter-term goals like sprint goals and intermediate-term goals like product goals.

Consistent use of empiricism and experimentation helps organizations achieve optimal outcomes based on intelligent adaptations.

Plans are often based on hopes, beliefs, and visions. However, upon inspection, supporting data is often absent or contradictory. Data that could support a plan is often inconveniently absent, or when present it is at odds with the beliefs.

*****

In our industry, EBM is revolutionary, but it is essential to avoid fads based on marketing assertions. This book was written by people who have helped others learn how to use software and other complex products more wisely. Read and learn.

Scrum has been out for 30 years. Using Scrum and EBM entails paradigm shifts that only those with a serious work ethic seem willing to undertake, but these shifts are the only way to move forward in a complex world.

Scrum On!

Ken Schwaber

FOREWORD BY DAVE WEST

The one reality for organizations and people in the twenty-first century is uncertainty. And this uncertainty leads to complexity. Digital technology amplifies both the uncertainty and our ability to perceive it. Ultimately, that means organizations and individuals need to be more agile to adapt in response to our changing understanding of the world around us. For Scrum. org, agility is defined as three basic ideas:

- An empirical approach to work. That means breaking work into small increments, delivering those increments, and learning from that process and associated outcomes.
- Empowered teams. That means allowing the teams doing the work to own the how and the what.
- Continuous improvement. This is the belief that everything can be improved.

These three ideas are simple, but they are surprisingly tricky to implement. From my experience, the challenge can be defined as the disconnect between work and value. In the past 100 years, people, teams, and organizations have concentrated on efficiently delivering work. Percent complete, on-time, and on-budget metrics are the traditional standards by which teams are measured.

But teams find questions such as, "Why is this more important than that" and "Why does the user need that" much harder to answer. That in itself is not a problem if the result of the work is valuable.

Here's the problem: Deciding what is valuable work is more complex and more challenging as you increase complexity and uncertainty. That is even harder the further away from the work the decision is being made. Aligning and focusing teams on the why is the fundamental first step to agility. It allows teams to do the work that makes the most sense and bridges the gap to purpose, which authors such as Dan Pink and Simon Sinek highlight as crucial to motivation and better outcomes.

Value is the not-so-secret sauce of effective agile transformations. Similarly, buying a poster that reads, "Customer first," does not make your company a customer-first organization. Saying that your agile transformation focuses on value does not mean you are aligned or measured on value. And one person's value is another person's activity.

That is why the ideas of Evidence-Based Management (EBM) are so helpful. EBM supplies a framework for effectively putting goals and supporting measures in place to provide direction to teams and organizations on their journey to value. They focus not on the motion of the organization but on the outcomes. At the heart of EBM are the customers and the organization's ability to serve them.

Ken Schwaber, the co-creator of Scrum, created EBM in response to a simple question his customers asked: "How agile are we?" EBM was inspired by evidence-based medicine, which applies the scientific method to organize and apply current data to improve healthcare decisions. Evidence-based medicine tries to answer clinical questions for a patient. It provides a framework for questions about the customer and the organization. EBM focuses on four key value areas (KVAs): current value, unrealized value, time to market, and ability to innovate. Each organization or team will find its own goals and metrics to explore those areas, and those measures will change over time. Also, notice that the answer to the question, "How agile are we?" provided by EBM is not directly about agile but rather agility's impact on value.

As you can imagine, Ken's answer was often met with a confused look. Agility should never be the reason for the change but instead the answer to delivering more value and managing the unknown. EBM focuses on the outcomes, not the mechanics of the process or approach. These KVAs should provide data that then drives improvements, which in turn, drives changes to the data. And thus, the cycle continues.

The ideas of EBM are simple, but the challenge is applying them. Most organizations are good at measuring motion, but transitioning this to value can take time and effort. That is why a practical book on applying EBM is valuable.

In this book, Patricia, Todd, Ryan, and Kurt provide a practical guide on how to use EBM. They start with goals and purpose and then move into effectiveness, expectations, and noise vs. signal chapters. Finally, they discuss EBM at the product, portfolio, and organizational levels. EBM is a valuable tool for product teams, but you can also apply it at the organizational level as part of an enterprise agile transformation program. Throughout this book, the authors describe a pragmatic approach to adoption using examples to cite how organizations that have many challenges can still gain something from this approach. That is the great thing about EBM. It does not require wholesale change but can be applied in the small or large. Of course, the most significant return on EBM is when it helps drive organizational change. But EBM can achieve value at whatever level you are applying the change. These principles can help teams, products, portfolios, and organizations.

Even after more than six years of applying EBM at Scrum.org, I still found this book usable and compelling. I enjoyed the case studies and examples and often saw my experiences in these stories. Even when you know Scrum, have lots of experience implementing it, and understand the concepts of EBM, changing your mindset after 25+ years of activity and motion focus takes work. Throughout this book, the authors highlight the importance of balance—not just balance in focus between the different key value areas, but balance in implementation. Teams often have different stakeholder needs, and EBM can be a great vehicle to balance those sometimes conflicting requirements.

After all, everything affects the customer. It just requires an understanding of the timeframe, lens, or focus.

Good luck on your voyage. I hope EBM is a helpful compass.

Scrum On!

Dave West

PREFACE

More than thirty years ago, Ken Schwaber and Jeff Sutherland created an approach to software development and delivery they called *Scrum*, after the huddle-like teaming practice used in rugby. At the time, software development teams struggled to deliver complex software systems. Simple programs were easy, but somewhere, things fell apart as the work became more complex. Years-long, many-person initiatives failed to achieve results, with alarming regularity. Scrum helped these initiatives deliver working products in a series of increments.

The organizations in which teams using Scrum worked still had a problem: They looked at the development effort as simply a cost they wanted to minimize. They could not see the work for what it really was: an engine for creating value. They needed a new way to look at their development efforts and a new way to manage that focused on value, not simply cost and revenue. Building on ideas Ken borrowed from evidence-based medicine, the ideas embodied in EBM evolved.

For us, Evidence-Based Management (EBM) helps answer a fundamental question that teams and organizations struggle with: What is value?

Measuring value is not as easy as it might first seem. Organizations use profit (revenue – cost) as a proxy for value, but increasing profit makes a poor goal because it does not provide insight into what the organization should do to grow its profit. Better goals always involve providing something of value to customers. Things are valuable to customers when they satisfy their needs and help them achieve an outcome they value.

In our work with Scrum.org, we meet with many organizations at various waypoints on their agile journeys. One of the key questions we try to ask them is, "What are you trying to achieve with your agile initiative?" Of all the answers we get, one theme stands out: They want to go faster or be more responsive to change or new opportunities.

On the surface, that seems like a fine objective. What organization would not want to be more responsive? But at another level, merely going faster seems rather purposeless. That is why we always ask a second question: "What will you do when you can go faster?" And that is when we get puzzled expressions telling us they have not thought about that. Our version of the answer is that the true goals of an organization have to do with delivering value to customers. Being more responsive to customer needs is important, but first it is necessary to understand those needs.

Delivering value sustainably means focusing on more than just the value that customers experience. It also must include the means of delivering that value: the organization's effectiveness in delivering value and the speed at which it can respond to new information. Organizations claiming their goal is to become faster and more responsive are right. Still, they also need to think more strategically about what they will do when they can deliver value to customers more quickly.

This book helps organizations achieve a more balanced perspective on value. It elevates and illuminates strategic customer-focused goals, but it also uses short feedback loops to quickly try new ideas that might improve the customer's experience. We want to help organizations deliver value to customers using those same feedback loops.

Lest this book seems too focused on organizational themes, we also have a more personal purpose in writing it. In our work, we also see a lot of people who aren't engaged in the work they do because they feel disconnected from the goals of the organization, which, in turn, are disconnected from customer value. Their work seems pointless and purposeless. We have seen how working toward meaningful goals is life-changing, and we want to help others find their purpose. Seeing how one's work is connected to important customer and societal goals motivates and provides meaning in ways that "enhancing shareholder value" never will.

For organizations and employees that think agility simply means "go faster," we hope this book will restore purpose to agile initiatives that have "lost their why." We hope that it will help them reconnect with their customers using frequent feedback and help them continually and systematically improve their ability to make progress toward meaningful goals. If these goals resonate with you, we encourage you to read on.

Patricia, Todd, Kurt, and Ryan

Register your copy of *Unlocking Business Agility with Evidence-Based Management: Satisfy Customers and Improve Organizational Effectiveness* on the InformIT site for convenient access to updates and/or corrections as they become available. To start the registration process, go to informit.com/register and log in or create an account. Enter the product ISBN (9780138244576) and click Submit. Look on the Registered Products tab for an Access Bonus Content link next to this product, and follow that link to access any available bonus materials. If you would like to be notified of exclusive offers on new editions and updates, please check the box to receive email from us.

ACKNOWLEDGMENTS

Ideas are not developed in isolation, and neither are books. We owe a debt of gratitude to the many people, teams, and organizations that have supported us in developing and furthering the ideas of Evidence-Based Management (EBM).

Thank you to Ken Schwaber, who created the idea of EBM based on his experience working with organizations, and Chris Schwaber for exposing us to the ideas of evidence-based medicine.

Thank you to the EBM Scrum.org community, who helped us refine EBM by experimenting with it and offering valuable feedback we used to update the EBM Guide and create the Professional EBM Course. Thanks to Lorenz Cheung, Chris Conlin, Karel Deman, Nic Easton, Magdalena Firlit, Ralph Jocham, Ken Kwan, Sergey Makarkin, Don McGreal, Mark Noneman, Simon Reindl, Will Seele, Ravi Verma, Wojciech Walczak, and Mark Wavle.

In addition to the Professional Scrum Trainer community of Scrum.org, thank you to the people who have translated the EBM Guide into their local languages. We appreciate how much this spreads our ideas globally.

This book would not be possible in its current form without the feedback of Glaudia Califano and Will Seele. It also would not exist without the support of our friends, colleagues, and family. Our deepest thanks!

ABOUT THE AUTHORS

Patricia Kong helps organizations thrive in a complex world by focusing on enterprise innovation, leadership, and teams. She is a people advocate and fascinated by organizational behaviors and misbehaviors. She is co-author of both *The Nexus Framework for Scaling Scrum* (Addison-Wesley, 2017) and *Facilitating Professional Scrum Teams* (Addison-Wesley, 2024).

Todd Miller has practical experience as a Scrum Master, Product Owner, Software Developer, and Agile coach on a variety of technical and creative projects across a multitude of industries. He has been a professional Scrum trainer with Scrum.org since 2016.

Kurt Bittner has been delivering working products in short, feedback-driven cycles for more than 40 years, and has helped many organizations do the same. He is particularly interested in helping people form strong, self-organizing, high-performance teams that deliver solutions that customers love, and helping organizations use empirical feedback to achieve customer outcome-focused goals.

Ryan Ripley is a Professional Scrum Trainer with Scrum.org, and has experience as a software developer, manager, director, and Scrum Master at various Fortune 500 companies in the medical device, wholesale, and financial services industries. He is the host of "Agile for Humans," the top agile podcast on iTunes. He recently co-wrote *Fixing Your Scrum: Practical Solutions for Common Scrum Problems* (Pragmatic Bookshelf, 2022).

INTRODUCTION

Many organizations practice color-coding projects to show their status. Green means everything on the project is going fine, yellow means the project needs some help, and red means the project is failing. Most projects start as green. Changing an in-flight project to yellow or, even worse, to red, often causes a three-alarm fire. Most project managers and teams do not want that level of management attention, so many projects that look "officially" green to the outside world are yellow or red on the inside. We call this phenomenon a *watermelon project*.

Organizations can function just like watermelon projects. From the outside, they look healthy and successful, but on the inside, they struggle to deliver anything valuable to their customers. These organizations tend to have cultures of *false positivism*, in which everything is always "great!" and where any signs of less-than-complete enthusiasm can be career-ending. They operate on a narrative of ever-and-ever greater success, with no humbling missteps, and any shortfalls in performance are either covered up or blamed on a convenient scapegoat.

The problem these organizations face is that they are unable to learn from experience; therefore, they cannot respond to unexpected events. During a long string of random occurrences, they may be able to avoid the consequences of their inability to learn and adapt, but they cannot avoid it forever.

In the end, their inability to learn hampers them and ends the string of success they may have achieved to date.

Many organizations today claim they want to be more responsive to customer needs and competitor challenges. They often express these claims by investing heavily in internal change initiatives that, once completed, result in a more customer-centric mindset. They invest heavily to do so, not knowing whether they have changed anything at all.

Leading consulting firms and tool vendors have built businesses to perpetuate these hopes by promising easy paths to a customer-first mindset that offers responsiveness, efficiency, and speed. However, after the initial fanfare, these initiatives almost always lose focus and support, devolving into shallow ways of working that feel different but produce no better results. After millions spent and years lost, organizations find that their customer-centric journeys lead them, more or less, right back to where they started. The thing we see often that has changed is that they have new management who end up starting similar initiatives.

We have found that most of these customer-centric initiatives sow their seeds of failure at their start: by making the goal "to improve the process." Having better processes is not a goal; it is a means to an end. Better processes are really just shorthand for learning while navigating the unknown in pursuit of a goal. It is an approach for trying ideas, getting rapid feedback on those ideas, inspecting that feedback, and adapting plans for the next step based on what was learned. Feedback is essential. This is where watermelon organizations find themselves stuck: Their culture requires that things always look good, but most learning stems from things not going as planned and having to understand why. These organizations are trapped by their inability to see things the way they are, as opposed to how they want them to be.

PURPOSE OF THIS BOOK

Our purpose in writing this book is to help organizations find their true purpose, improve their ability to reach their goals, and build a culture of trust and transparency that allows them to learn from their experiences.

For us, an organization's purpose is to deliver value to customers. Many organizations say that they are customer-focused because it sounds good for them to say it. But for many, these words lack meaning because organizations do not measure customer outcomes. They have no idea if what they do creates customer value. An organization that has no idea whether what it does is valuable lacks the information it needs to be responsive. An organization that does not know whether what it does is valuable wastes its time being faster or more efficient.

However, organizations seem to have lost their way in the modern world. They believe in the certainty of their plans and that every deviation from the plan is a sign of failure. They view the organization as a machine for creating and executing plans instead of looking at it as a responsive organism, attentive to the changes in its environment. In a world of uncertainties, organizations need to be responsive organisms, not rigid machines incapable of reinventing themselves every day based on new information.

This book aims to change all that. It uses a framework developed by Scrum.org called *Evidence-Based Management*[1], or *EBM*. You do not have to know anything about EBM to read this book. In some ways, EBM is nothing new; it is simply the *scientific method*, simplified and applied to helping organizations achieve their goals under conditions of uncertainty. People have been applying the ideas behind EBM for hundreds—even thousands—of years when they solve novel problems using experimentation.

Throughout this book, we present stories and experiences that illustrate how you can apply EBM to set better goals and then leverage empiricism to achieve those goals using feedback, learning, and evidence. The situations in these stories will be familiar to you. They will present ideas you can try in your own organization to help it become more responsive.

But first we will look at what EBM is and how it works.

---

1. https://www.scrum.org/resources/evidence-based-management-guide

A BRIEF INTRODUCTION TO EBM

EBM is an empirical approach that helps organizations use experimentation and rapid feedback to progress toward goals (see Figure Intro 1). This path is not always obvious or straightforward, but that is a benefit. In a complex and changing world, the path toward goals is always uncertain. EBM helps organizations use new data to adapt their course toward their goals.

Figure Intro 1 EBM helps organizations set and reach strategic goals in uncertain times.

EBM breaks down *strategic goals* into smaller goals that, when achieved, help the organization measure whether it is making progress toward strategic goals. To this end, EBM talks about three levels of goals:

- *Strategic goals* are important things the organization wants to achieve. Strategic goals are so big and far away, with many uncertainties along the journey, that the organization must use empiricism to achieve them. Because the strategic goal is aspirational, and the path to it is uncertain, the organization needs a series of realistic targets, like intermediate goals, discussed next.
- *Intermediate goals* are achievements indicating that the organization is on the path to its strategic goal. The path to the intermediate goal is often still somewhat uncertain but not completely unknown. Organizations also need immediate tactical goals to take smaller, focused steps toward strategic and intermediate goals.
- *Immediate tactical goals* are critical near-term objectives toward which a team or group of teams can work over a short period ranging from a few weeks to a month.

To progress toward the strategic goal, organizations run experiments that involve forming hypotheses intended to advance them toward their current intermediate goal. As they run these experiments and gather results, they use the evidence they obtain to evaluate their goals and determine their next steps to advance toward these goals.

In forming goals, EBM also distinguishes between different goal targets:

- **Activities:** These are things that people in the organization do, such as perform work, go to meetings, have discussions, write code, create reports, and attend conferences.
- **Outputs:** These are things that the organization produces, such as product releases (including features), reports, defect reports, and product reviews.
- **Outcomes:** These are desirable things a customer or user of a product experiences.

Goals based on activities and outputs are ineffective and demotivating. They reduce teams' ability to devise creative solutions by telling them what to do and how to work. Goals are best expressed in terms of the customer outcomes that the organization wants to achieve.

And what about internal goals, like improving profit? Although goals like these are important, ignoring customers does not help an organization figure out what it needs to do for current or prospective customers to make more money. We believe that by focusing on satisfying unmet customer needs, the organization will make more money.

Empiricism and experimentation fit in the experiment loop. Teams delivering value to customers consider customer needs, identify things they think will help those customers, develop and deliver a small increment of value to test their ideas, gather feedback from customers on what they delivered, and then inspect the feedback to decide if they should continue to improve that idea. The move on to another idea if the idea was not valuable or what the teams delivered was sufficient.

Feedback is also helpful in evaluating goals. The organization might find that things they thought customers needed are not crucial to them after all. And the organization might find new customer needs they did not understand before. This means the organization might need to adjust goals at all levels.

Along with goals and the experiment loop, EBM introduces four key value areas (KVAs) that organizations use to consider what value they are delivering and could pursue, as well as their ability to do so (see Figure Intro 2). This book unfolds how organizations can use the different KVAs to focus their decisions and improve their capabilities.

Evidence-Based Management and Key Value Areas

Market Value

What is the potential value that the organization can achieve?

Unrealized Value (UV)

Current Value (CV)

What value is the organization currently delivering?

Agility
Business Value

How effective is the organization at improving value?

Ability to Innovate (A2I)

Time to Market (T2M)

How long does it take to deliver new value?

Organizational Capability

Figure Intro 2 KVAs in a nutshell.

The Evidence-Based Management Guide defines each KVA as follows:

- **Current value (CV):** The value the product delivers today.
- **Unrealized value (UV):** The potential future value that can be realized if the organization meets the needs of all potential customers or users.
- **Time-to-market (T2M):** The organization's ability to quickly deliver new capabilities, services, or products.
- **Ability to innovate (A2I):** The effectiveness of an organization in delivering new capabilities that might better meet customer needs.

Within these KVAs, organizations can develop, inspect, and adapt their measurements, known as key value measures (KVMs), as they run experiments. They use the KVMs to gain information and evidence.

This is not all there is to say about EBM, but it is enough to get started. We will explore these ideas more fully in subsequent chapters.

WHO SHOULD READ THIS BOOK

This book is primarily targeted at middle-level and upper-middle-level managers who are responsible for guiding the organization toward its goals.

It is for those who are close enough to the work to understand how teams actually function and close enough to the executives who typically shape the organization's strategic goals to have influence on the creation and refinement of those goals. For these people, the book depicts organizational challenges and alternative solutions to help them improve.

Team members will also benefit from Chapters 2 and 3 as they look for ways to improve their own ability to achieve goals. The scenarios presented and discussed there will be valuable to team members, apart from whether they have organizational support for improving. Improving their ability to achieve goals may help them gain attention and support for the changes described elsewhere in this book.

This is not a book that presents a process for transforming organizations. If you are looking for that, you will be disappointed, although we have found the ideas presented herein transformative. By setting outcome-oriented goals, forming experiments, measuring the results, inspecting the results, and adapting their next steps accordingly, organizations can achieve remarkable results. Seeking goals using empiricism is a simple yet powerful approach, but there is no magic to it. Success comes from diligently applying the ideas, not from the ideas themselves.

How This Book is Organized

This book is organized around an extensive set of case studies that illustrate how EBM can help organizations deal with common challenges. Rather than creating a single case study, we share different organizational case studies. Although the case studies are based on real experiences, we have simplified and anonymized them to make them easier to understand and to focus each one on a single learning goal.

- **Chapter 1: Finding Purpose** describes how organizations can use goals to express their strategy in ways that connect the work they do to things that matter to customers and better engage employees in making those connections.

- **Chapter 2: Using Empericism to Progress Toward Goals** describes how to align short- and medium-term goals with strategic goals and how to use feedback to seek toward those goals, measure progress, and then adapt both the approach and the goal based on feedback.

- **Chapter 3: Becoming (More) Effective** describes how teams can use feedback to improve their ability to deliver to customers.

- **Chapter 4: Managing and Overcoming Expectations** describes how organizations can use feedback to stimulate and inform better conversations about improving organizational performance, focusing on changing the management system and the culture so it can embrace and act upon new information.

- **Chapter 5: Separating the Signal from the Noise** describes how to decide what measures to use, how to interpret feedback, and how to use that feedback to decide what to consider next.

- **Chapter 6: Applying EBM at the Product Level** describes how teams can use EBM to better connect with their customers by delivering products and services that improve customer outcomes and the team's ability to deliver those improved outcomes.

- **Chapter 7: Applying EBM at the Portfolio Level** describes how organizations can make the hard choices and trade-offs between different products and services based on feedback from customers.

- **Chapter 8: Applying EBM at the Organizational Level** describes how to reshape the organization to better take advantage of feedback from customers and the market, including how to create an organization that can reconfigure itself to better respond to feedback. We tackle these topics last because we have found that organizations change from the bottom-up, not the other way around. Changing an entire organization means starting in pockets, testing and proving ideas, and then expanding.

How to Read This Book

This book presents a logical progression of ideas, illustrated by short vignettes that illustrate things we have learned in working with real teams and organizations. The first time through this book, we recommend reading it cover-to-cover. The case studies build upon one another, and the earlier ones set the context for the later ones. After you have read this book once, you will probably want to return to sections that are particularly meaningful to your organization and its unique challenges. You may want to buy a package of sticky notes so you can flag discussions that are important to you.

FINDING PURPOSE

It's August and the start of the Medical Device Company's annual planning process. Cindy, the company's CEO, sends an email to Medical Device Company's executives to share her new strategic goal:

> We need to regain the competitive edge from our competitors. We must show that we can release new innovations faster than any other company. To that end, we need to patent and release a new knee replacement technology next year. In the interest of showing positive returns to our shareholders, this product also needs to be net-positive by the second half of the year.

The email continues, requesting the executive team to individually prepare strategies toward this strategic goal:

> I am excited about our future, but we can only do this if we work together. I would like to see your plans and timelines for this new knee replacement technology. My instinct tells me that this will send our company into the stratosphere. I hope you all are as excited as I am.

Soon after Cindy sends the email, company-wide meetings fill calendars at all levels of the organization as plans are created to fulfill Cindy's new strategic goal. Executives pull their direct reports into the conversation, and directors pull in employees. Separate teams spend hours brainstorming and identifying the risks and the viability of achieving Cindy's new objective.

Teams finish their proposals and offer plans, but many question how valuable and achievable these ideas are, especially in such a short time period.

In January, at the special company kick-off meeting, Cindy and the CFO share the projected sales numbers and other market figures. They are very excited and want everyone else to understand how vital this work is to the company's future. This new product will help the Medical Device Company regain a competitive edge in the industry and become the market leader. But sideways glances and water cooler chat tell another story. Team members quietly question how they can continue with the number of projects they are already working on while launching this new product. Will the Medical Device Company hire more staff? Will that cut into profits? Will everyone work longer hours and wait to see if the product is well received to get a raise?

This scenario plays out every year in countless organizations. A senior executive proposes an initiative that will lead the organization to "success." Executives translate this initiative into aspirational plans, and managers and their teams scramble to inject reality into those plans. The organization measures success in simple terms: Did they deliver the things that the senior executive desires, did they perform better than the competition, and did the company make a lot of money?

What happens next is also typical: People in the organization already work at their limits supporting existing products. They have doubts about the achievability of the new plan, but they know that existing customers still need help and support. As the year progresses, the new initiative stumbles, and management pressures teams to deliver. Quality, customer satisfaction, and morale suffer.

Long before the end of the year, finger-pointing on why the new initiative has failed has already started. The person in charge of the new product is replaced, and the initiative is reorganized. The assumption is that poor execution and a lack of commitment are why the company cannot get anything done; plans and goals remain largely unquestioned by management. This cycle keeps repeating, though the products and the specifics vary slightly. Despite all this effort and constant refocusing, the company's performance never seems to improve.

Something needs to be fixed. This organization has lost its purpose.

REDISCOVERING PURPOSE

Most organizations do things for a reason. They do not exist simply to make money or employ people, although, for commercial businesses, profit is always a motivator. People often find and go to organizations because they want to see some change in the world. They want to help achieve the vision the company is chasing. The organization they found reflects their unique way of looking at the world and the unique approach they will use to achieve their vision; this is their *mission*. From these foundations, organizations form goals that they believe, when they are achieved, will represent progress toward the future state they would like to see (see Figure 1.1).

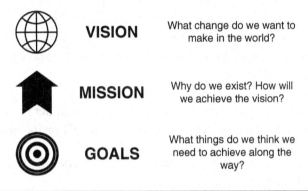

Figure 1.1 Organizations form to achieve a vision. Their unique approach to achieving this is expressed in their mission. Goals help organizations understand whether they are making progress toward their vision.

Creating a vision, mission, and supporting strategy is the focus of company founders or executive leadership and is outside the scope of this book.[1] We focus on goals—specifically strategic, intermediate, and immediate tactical—because we find that organizations get lost in the pursuit of goals. They forget who they are and what they are seeking.

---

1. Peter Drucker's article on organizational missions is an interesting starting point for those interested in learning more about this topic: https://www.drucker.institute/wp-content/uploads/2018/08/Reading_Drucker-on-Mission.pdf.

GOALS

Recall our definition of strategic goals from the Introduction:

> *Strategic goals are important things the organization wants to achieve. Strategic goals are so big and far away, with many uncertainties along the journey, that the organization must use empiricism. Because the strategic goal is aspirational and the path to it is uncertain, the organization needs a series of realistic targets.*

Like the Medical Device Company's company in our scenario, many organizations focus their strategic goals on factors that are important to the company but not to customers. They want to improve profit and beat their competitors, but they have forgotten their customers. They have lost sight of what it takes to create value for those customers. Creating value for customers is the foundation for all other kinds of business performance, including a commitment from employees.

Customer: anyone who gets value from the product or service you are delivering, whether that person is its receiver ("user") or its buyer ("payer").

To better explain this concept of value, consider the four types of measures often used to form goals:

- **Activities:** These are *things that people do*, such as perform work, go to meetings, have discussions, write code, create reports, design graphics, and attend conferences.
- **Outputs:** These are *things that people produce*, such as product releases (including features), reports, defect reports, graphics, and product reviews.
- **Outcomes:** These are *desirable things that a customer of a product experiences*. They represent some new or improved capability that the customer was not able to achieve before, such as being able to travel to a destination faster than before or being able to earn or save more money.
- **Impacts:** These are *things that the organization achieves*, such as showing a profit or a loss. Impacts are important, but they arise from doing valuable things for customers and cannot be achieved independently of delivering customer value.

Achieving outcomes should always be the real goal of producing outputs or performing activities. The outputs and activities may be a means to an end, but they are never the end themselves. Expressing objectives in terms of outputs is bad because it can lead to micromanaging people to produce something that does not help the organization move closer to the objective. Expressing objectives in terms of activities is even worse: it micromanages people by telling them what to do.

The path to achieving a vision is almost always indirect. To achieve it, organizations need to get customers to do things, such as buying their products or using their services. For customers to be willing to do things, they must obtain some benefit. They need to achieve some *outcome* that they desire. Ultimately, then, for the organization to succeed, goals need to be directly or indirectly focused on *customer outcomes*.

The problem that the Medical Device Company faces in our opening scenario is that its strategic goal is expressed in terms of *impacts* (beating competitors and making money) and *outputs* (producing a specific product). Although beating competitors and making money is important, it is unclear what the new product the CEO is pushing for will do for customers. The CEO's plan will invest a lot of money in something that may or may not happen, and that is pretty risky.

What is missing, in our view, is a set of short-, medium-, and long-term goals that will tell the company whether it is on track to achieve its vision. What it has, instead, is fairly typical: plans that dictate a set of *activities* that will produce a set of *outputs*. As one of our former colleagues used to put it, these *activities* and *outputs* have lost their *"why."* They have lost track of the *outcomes* that customers want. They *assume* that the new product will deliver unique outcomes that customers cannot achieve in any other way, but they do not know that for certain. If they are wrong about their assumptions, and most organizations are, they will spend a lot of time and effort while achieving very little.[2]

---

2. See https://www.infoq.com/articles/empiricism-business-agility/ for a discussion and supporting research on why most product ideas don't actually improve customer experiences.

Should goals be S.M.A.R.T.?

SMART describes a set of criteria that are frequently applied to goals, asserting that goals should be:

- **Specific:** Target a specific area for improvement.
- **Measurable:** Quantify or at least suggest an indicator of progress.
- **Assignable:** Specify who will do it.
- **Realistic:** State what results can realistically be achieved, given available resources.
- **Time-bound:** Specify when the result(s) can be achieved.

SMART goals have permeated many organizations, with many people accepting that a good goal must meet the SMART criteria. But is this always a good approach?

In some interpretations, the "A" in SMART means goals should be assignable, whereas in others, the "A" means goals should be attainable. We prefer to ignore the attainable interpretation because attainable is the same as realistic.

In our work, we have found that good goals are always specific and measurable; if they are not, they cannot provide useful targets toward which organizations can work. Vague goals whose achievement cannot be measured are merely empty aspirations. But the other SMART criteria are, in our opinion, outdated and even dangerous because they encourage a simplistic and short-sighted approach to management.

Many organizations pursue agile approaches because they are interested in improving their speed of delivery; they intuitively sense that they must be more responsive to changes in customer preferences and threats that competitors pose. Although delivery speed is important, focusing only on speed misses the bigger opportunity, which is to engage with customers more deeply. The real benefit of improving delivery speed is increasing the frequency at which customer sentiments can be measured.

In addition to speed, many organizations focus on increasing the rate of output of their people, often expressed in measures like velocity. The focus is well intentioned, but this attention is also largely misplaced. Instead of looking at how much output the team produces, organizations should focus on how much value the team produces. Viewed from the customer's perspective, there is no connection between output and value experienced.

To better understand unmet customer needs, teams need to be able to run experiments about value quickly, gather information about whether those experiments meet customer needs, and then adapt their future plans quickly. In this context, it is not delivery speed that is important but learning speed. Teams can improve their performance in this respect by reducing waste and interruptions that steal their attention from the learning goals they have set, as expressed in their immediate tactical goals. Over time, achieving these value-oriented, learning-oriented will help a team make progress toward its intermediate goals and ultimately toward its strategic goals, which are both usually expressed in terms of fulfilling unmet customer needs.

HOW GOALS AND MEASURES INFLUENCE BEHAVIORS

Expressing goals in terms of outputs often leads to micromanaging people to produce something that is not guaranteed to help the organization move closer to its desired outcome. Expressing goals in terms of activities is even worse because it micromanages people by telling them exactly what to do and when to do it. Both output and activity-oriented goals lead to a disconnect between the people doing the work and the value it intends to bring to the customer.

To explore this, consider an activity-oriented goal for the sales organization of a consulting company. Suppose management sees a downtick in revenue in the past quarter and feels as though the sales organization needs to acquire more new customers. Management decides to create a goal for the new quarter for the sales organization that states the following: "Triple the number of new client interactions through email or phone." What unintentional behaviors might happen because of this goal? Is that resulting behavior positive?

Micromanaging people is counterproductive and demoralizing. It presumes that people lack the competence to decide on the best way to achieve a goal. In nearly all cases, the people closest to the work are better able to make decisions about how to achieve a goal because they have the most information about available alternatives; this is known as bottom-up intelligence. When organizations free their people to contribute using their knowledge, experience, and passion, they achieve better results. For this potential to be fulfilled, both the top (that does understand the context) and the bottom (that understands the product) need to share critical knowledge with one another.

The connection between goals, their measures, and the behavior of people in an organization has many components, which makes it quite a complex relationship. Beyond the old truism that "what gets measured gets done," a goal can be either motivating or demotivating. Figure 1.2 describes the interaction between goals, the measures used to assess progress toward those goals, and how that affects behavior.

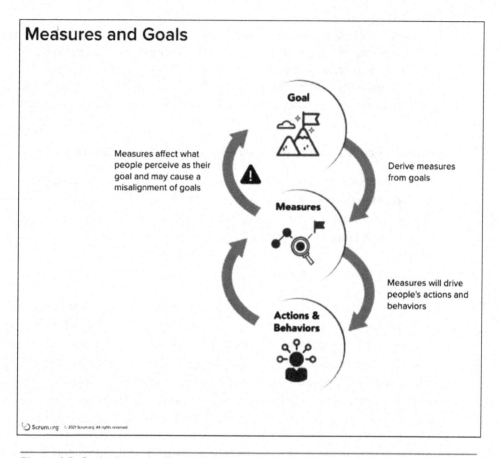

Figure 1.2 Goals ultimately affect both how people work and what they do here.

Goals expressed in terms of activities usually ensure that those activities are completed. You have to be certain that performing that work will lead to some valuable results. More often, goals expressed as activities lead to disengaged employees who go through the motions.

We believe that goals expressed in terms of outputs have a similar problem to goals expressed as activities. Whoever creates the goal must be certain that producing the specified output will lead to some valuable result. This is the trap many product managers fall into when they dictate that specific features need to be delivered: they assume they are valuable. The result is disengagement. A team will simply focus on delivering the dictated feature rather than thinking deeply about what customers might really care about.

Goals expressed in terms of outcomes tend to engage people. Freed from dictated work or outputs, they think more deeply about what customers care about, and they have opportunities to find better ways to solve customer problems. When close to their customers, their greater insights lead to better solutions.

The lack of customer-focused strategic goals has other side effects. When team members work on things that have no connection to strategic goals, not only are they less intrinsically motivated, but the executives in the organization have little idea whether the organization is doing anything valuable. They may know that people performed certain work or that they produced certain outputs, but they do not know whether any of that was valuable to customers. To do better, the organization must refocus its purpose on things that matter to customers.

Why "On Time, On Scope, and Under Budget" Is Not Success

Decades of accepted best practices in managing projects have instilled in managers the idea that projects are successful when they deliver—on time—everything that was on the approved scope within the approved budget. This would be true if the project were building something well understood, like a building or a bridge. Civilization has thousands of years of experience building structures; we know what they are and how to build them. We can describe the structures that must be delivered in minute detail.

The "on-time, on-scope, within-budget" approach fails when dealing with new problems. The less the problem is understood, or the more novel the solution, the worse the traditional approach performs. Consider treating a new disease. How long will an effective treatment take to develop? How much will it cost to develop? What should the treatment consist of? At the onset of the disease, we can answer none of these questions.

Many business problems, especially those that deal with improving customer experiences, are similarly hard to scope. Customer needs are often hard to understand and are constantly changing. Customers learn and adapt because the world in which they live is constantly changing, and competitors are constantly delivering new solutions that change customer experiences. A company can build a new product exactly to specification, to an aggressive schedule, and within a tight budget and still fail if customers do not respond positively to the product.

So what is the solution? Think about how we respond to new diseases. People work in small increments. They diagnose the problem. They form hypotheses about possible solutions. They run experiments to test their hypotheses. They gather data, refine their problem understanding, and form new hypotheses. As a civilization, we have hundreds of years of experience with this approach. For novel problems, this approach works.

HOW TO REDISCOVER PURPOSE

Customers buy a product for a lot of reasons, most of which boil down to "this product is better than the alternatives I have." Simply being the best of bad alternatives leaves the organization vulnerable to competitors. But simply being better than competitors is not a very good goal either. It means you are letting your competitors lead, and when you do that, you will always be playing catch-up.

A better way to understand customer needs is to consider their *satisfaction gap*: the difference between their current experience and their desired experience (see Figure 1.3).

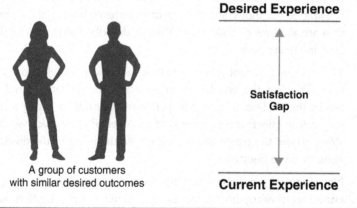

Figure 1.3 Consider satisfaction gaps to understand value creation opportunities.

The concept of a satisfaction gap is closely related to *Unrealized Value*—or the potential value that the organization *could* deliver to its customers. Different groups of customers will have different satisfaction gaps. The Unrealized Value for the entire organization is the economic value of closing all satisfaction gaps that customers experience. The organization only creates value when it does something that reduces a satisfaction gap for a customer or set of customers.

Unrealized Value (UV): The potential future value that *could be* realized if the organization meets the needs of all potential customers or users.

Consider again the goals set forth by Cindy at Medical Device Corporation:

We need to regain the competitive edge from our competitors. We must show that we can release new innovations faster than any other company. To that end, we need to patent and release a new knee replacement technology next year. In the interest of showing positive returns to our shareholders, this product also needs to be net positive by the second half of the year.

Will any goals expressed in Cindy's statement reduce a satisfaction gap? Maybe, but her goals do not say anything about customers, and they do not measure customer experiences. If the organization achieves Cindy's stated goals and reduces Unrealized Value, it will be a happy accident, not intentional.

When trying to rediscover purpose, initiate a conversation around the Unrealized Value your customers want to experience. Unrealized Value helps an organization maximize the value that it realizes from a product or service over time.

CLOSING SATISFACTION GAPS CREATES VALUE

Ultimately, an organization's vision is an expression of some sort of satisfaction gap. Closing that gap achieves the vision. But closing the gap is usually not a short-term thing. Organizations exist because achieving the vision takes time and perseverance. That is why strategic goals generally work best when they are framed in terms of Unrealized Value. Customers will not buy your product or use your service unless it closes a satisfaction gap. As a result, organizations have to focus on understanding and closing satisfaction gaps (i.e., reducing *Unrealized Value*) to make progress toward achieving their vision. There are several reasons for this:

- **Organizations only create value when they improve the outcomes that their customers experience.** They cannot create value for customers by reducing costs, becoming more efficient, or even delivering faster, although improving these things may help them deliver value to customers.

- **Improving customer outcomes requires an organization to continually improve its ability to sense what customers want.** Customers are continually experiencing new things, and their desired outcomes and current experiences constantly change. Helping customers achieve their desired outcomes is typically a long, never-ending journey that requires an organization to engage with its customers and try new ideas continually.

- **Customer satisfaction gaps generally take time to close.** Significant satisfaction gaps result from big differences between what customers experience today and what they want to experience. They may require broad societal changes that are beyond any one organization's ability to control in the short run, or maybe even at all, or they may require significantly different choices to be available to customers, none of which can be changed overnight, or even over a single year.

To see how this works in practice, consider the strategic goals for Medical Device Corporation: being faster than competitors does not guarantee that what the company delivers to customers is useful. Even obtaining more patents does not guarantee that those patents result in meaningful changes in customer outcomes. And simply making a lot of money, while desirable, does not give anyone guidance on how to improve the lives of customers.

What would happen if Cindy set the company's goal to deliver the cheapest implant by the end of the following year, with no concern for customer/ patient outcomes? What if the company met that goal? What will happen to the company's reputation if customer outcomes start to suffer? In the medical device industry, negative patient outcomes often lead to lawsuits that can take a company down. Strategic goals matter; forgetting about the customer is a quick way to destroy shareholder value, not increase it.

What if Cindy took a different approach? Instead of telling the organization what she wants them to deliver, what if she talked about the outcomes she wants the organization's customers to experience? Consider the difference if Cindy framed Medical Device Corporation's strategic goal in the following message:

I believe if we focus, we can help our customers achieve better and more successful outcomes. Consider what they experience today. Traditionally, a hip or knee implant means a long recovery after surgery, followed by months of physical therapy. The older the patient, the longer the recovery time and physical therapy.

To put this in human terms, let me share with you the recent experience of a typical customer. Imagine a family gathering for the holidays. It is an idyllic scene until Grandma trips and falls and badly injures her hip. We all know how challenging this situation can be. But what if we could market a product enabling Grandma to be up and walking within a day of having surgery? What if she could go home and resume most of her prior activities within a week?

Expressing goals in terms of outcomes answers the question, "Why are you doing what you are doing?" in a precise way. It also makes the goal more concrete and easier to measure by providing a way to know if the goal is achieved. The goal may not be achievable, but it is possible to know if it was achieved. The original goal presented at the start of this chapter is not specific enough to know if the organization has achieved it. How can an organization ever really know if it is better than its competitors or if it has produced the lowest-cost device? These measures are short term and not a good measure of how well the organization performs for its customers.

CUSTOMER-FOCUSED GOALS ENABLE AUTONOMY AND PURPOSE

Ample evidence shows that knowledge workers are motivated by, among other things, feeling that their work has meaning and purpose.[3] Customer-focused goals give them a sense that what they are working on matters in ways that simply "being more efficient" and "making more money" cannot.

Consider, again, the story about Medical Device Corporation. Feeling that one's work helps Grandma resume her normal life is powerfully motivating for the teams working on the new product and even for the other people in the organization supporting those teams. Organizations thrive on stories that help their employees feel connected to something larger than themselves.

Many employees are motivated by having a sense of autonomy and ownership. Goals that focus on customer outcomes also make it easier for employees to make decisions, providing them greater autonomy over their work. They can look at what they are doing and ask themselves, "Will this decision leave our customers better off? Will they improve the outcomes of our customers?" Being free to pursue ideas that improve customer outcomes is liberating and motivating and ultimately creates engaged employees who care about their customers and the organization.

Having customer-focused strategic goals helps in many ways. First, these types of goals align everything the company does with things customers care about. Second, they provide powerful motivation for employees to better meet the needs of customers. Third, they provide clearer measures for organizational success. Consider this example of a strategic goal that sounds customer-focused at first but has strayed from the path:

> Alpha is an insurance company that had a system to generate new quotes for a customer that was underperforming in several areas. It could take ten or more days for a customer to receive pricing and coverage information to

---

3. Dan Pink, in his book *Drive: The Surprising Truth About What Motivates Us*, provides a compelling argument that once basic financial needs are met, most people doing "knowledge work" are motivated by intrinsic factors such as guiding their own work, developing mastery of their craft, and contributing to achieving meaningful goals. For more information, see www.danpink.com/books/drive/.

choose between Alpha and one of its competitors. Alpha's internal process to issue a quote was also costly, confusing, and error-prone, requiring many departments to work together across hand-offs with no clear way to coordinate the work and no clear way to understand the status of a quote.

As frustration mounted, Terry, a vice president at Alpha, lobbied for funding to make the quoting process easier. Her elevator pitch for a new strategic goal follows:

> To create an automated quoting system that makes it easier to provide a quote to the customer.

She and her team estimated that this new endeavor would cost $10 million over three years. Terry lobbied hard for the new system. She spoke to multiple departments and collected measurements illustrating the pains each department experienced in the quoting process. Her objectiveness and presentation were convincing, and the Finance Committee quickly approved funding.

Two-and-a-half years later, the quoting system was finally in operation. The teams developing the quoting system had been thorough in their analysis; they had met frequently with each department to find ways to make their part of the quoting process more efficient. They even released new system versions frequently to obtain and adapt to feedback. On the surface, the new quoting system was a great success, and all the departments were much happier.

While developing the system, the development team identified more opportunities for improvement, so Terry lobbied again for additional funding. As she pitched the new improvement opportunities, the CEO asked how the new system had improved the time needed for customers to receive a quote. Terry had the team do some analysis to measure quote-to-customer because it was not something they had explicitly looked at. They were shocked to learn that customer quotes took about the same time as they did under the old system.

Terry and the team were in trouble.

This example illustrates what happens when a strategic goal loses sight of the customer. Terry's goal was stated as:

> *To create an automated quoting system that makes it easier to give a quote to the customer.*

The goal mentions the word *customer* but focuses on making things easier for Alpha, not better for their customers.

Because of this, two-and-a-half years and ten million dollars were spent on solving problems that may not have needed to be solved. If they had focused on reducing quote time to customers, they might not have needed much of what they developed. Their goal led them in the wrong direction. Worse, they had completely lost sight of the customer. Everyone forgot that the original problem they wanted to solve was reducing customer quote time.

What if Terry were to go back in time and rewrite the elevator pitch for the new strategic goal to something like this:

> *To create an automated quoting system that reduces the time it takes for the customer to receive a quote from us.*

This goal would motivate a completely different solution that would have to focus on eliminating wasteful steps and automating what they could not eliminate. Rather than creating a system that made the existing process easier, it would have approached the problem in ways that could have led to a better solution. This does not mean that the new process would have to be painful because, in eliminating wasteful steps, the pain each department experienced to produce a quote would also be reduced.

Centering strategic goals around the customer is vital to the success of an organization. If you do not do this, you may find yourself spending time and money on optimizing processes that have no real impact on the customer. It reminds us of the idiom, "polishing peanuts," when you work hard at something for little or no return. In other words, it means wasting time on work that will not yield reasonable value.

IMPROVING STRATEGIC GOALS

Organizations and the people in them are conditioned to frame strategic goals in terms of activities and outputs, and sometimes impacts, but rarely customer outcomes. Large organizations, split into functional departments, have largely lost sight of the customers outside of sales and marketing functions and some parts of product design. A big part of our work in helping customers frame better, more customer-focused strategic goals is to reconnect people in the larger organization with their customers. And this effort is not a one-time thing; it is a never-ending journey of rediscovery.

One of the first steps on this journey is to recognize that the organization's strategic goals are part of the problem. Signs of this include internally focused *strategic* goals, such as these:

- Improving productivity, becoming more efficient, or reducing cost
- Improving delivery speed or rate of output
- Improving revenues or profits or increasing shareholder returns
- Improving market share

All these things are important, and improving them will help the organization be more successful, but an organization that does not focus on improving its customers' experiences will not survive long enough for any of these things to matter. Put another way, excellent performance on the mentioned measures will not save the organization if a competitor can better satisfy the organization's customers.

ASK "WHY?" TO UNCOVER THE REAL OBJECTIVE

You can improve objectives expressed in outputs or activities by asking, "Why is that important?" If the answer is "because it will lead to something else," or some variant thereof, then the thing it will lead to is closer to the real objective, if not the real objective itself. You may have to apply this more than once to reach the real goal. To drill even deeper, you can follow that question with: "Can we achieve this goal and still not produce a positive change for our customers?" If achieving the goal will not improve your customer's experience, you must keep searching for your *real* goal.

Consider the example shown in Figure 1.4.

Weak Objective	Better Objective
• Make virtual training available for all courses by the end of the year	• Enable people to learn from wherever they are, whenever they need it

Figure 1.4 Improving a weak objective

The weak objective dictates an activity: creating and making available virtual training. A better objective is on the right. Students don't care whether they obtain training virtually or in person, but they would like to be able to learn whenever they need to, regardless of where they are located or what the course schedule is. This might lead to a different kind of learning than simply virtualizing existing courses.

Another example we often encounter is from organizations that, when asked why they want to be more agile, say that they want to "go faster," meaning that they want to release faster or get products to market faster. This objective fails the "why?" test. It is merely the means to some other goal, such as to be more responsive to customers or to competitor actions or to help customers obtain at least some value from a solution earlier.

Merely delivering faster is not enough to satisfy the goal of being more responsive; in addition to delivering faster, an organization must also "listen better" to better understand customer needs and to measure the change in customer outcomes resulting from delivering faster. Without this, organizations that deliver faster may be simply creating waste at a faster rate.

Because organizations are so conditioned to stating goals regarding activities or outputs, you will probably have to work hard, at least at first, to get to the "real" objective. Asking why will help you have better conversations about what the organization would like to achieve.

What About OKRs?

Objectives and key results (OKRs)[4] are a powerful tool for setting and measuring goals, but like all power tools, they can become dangerous in unskilled hands. When used in informed ways, they can improve focus and lift outcomes, but when mishandled, they can increase waste and inflict real damage upon the organizations that adopt them.

The basic idea behind OKRs is simple: It's a good idea to identify goals that you want to achieve and the measures that will indicate whether you have achieved those goals. No one would argue that this is a bad thing, at least if the goals are focused on conditions that the organization would like to achieve. Where OKRs can go "bad" is when they focus on merely producing things, and things can get really "ugly" when they focus on merely doing things. Objectives, in our view, should be focused on outcomes, as we have discussed.

Key results are indicators that tell people whether they are making progress toward a goal. Or at least that is the theory. The reality is that they are assumptions based on a presumed causal relationship between the key result and the objective, that if the organization achieves the key result, it will progress toward the objective.

Achieving a key result is generally regarded as positive, and failing to achieve the result is generally regarded as negative. This is flawed; achieving the key result might have no impact on achieving the objective. Failing to achieve a key result might not be a bad thing if achieving it is unrelated to achieving the objective; in fact, it might be a good thing if the organization learns something about the things that will help it achieve the objective.

It is better to regard key results as hypotheses about things that the organization can do to move toward the objective. Framing key results in this way makes it easier to discuss what the organization learned from the results, inspect these results, and adapt based on what the organization learns.

REFOCUS "INTERNAL" GOALS ON WHAT CUSTOMERS NEED TO EXPERIENCE

Sometimes just asking *why* isn't enough, as is the case when the organization's goals are all internally focused, such as "make more money," "increase profits," or "become more efficient or faster." Asking *why* helps, but you

---

4. See https://en.wikipedia.org/wiki/OKR for more information.

often find yourself at a dead-end answer like "make more money," which does not help the organization figure out what it needs to do to achieve the goal.

When you find yourself in this situation, try asking, "What will customers need to experience for us to achieve that goal?" It might be that *your* customers do not have a satisfaction gap, but a lot of potential customers out there do not know what you can do for them. In that case, making them aware of how you can help them might be your goal. In other words, you want to reach a set of potential customers who have a particular satisfaction gap that you can help them close.

In other cases, you might find that you need to deliver different products or services that will close the satisfaction gap of your own customers. You want to make your strategic goal about closing this satisfaction gap, while your intermediate and immediate tactical goals focus on specific experiments you are going to run with specific products or services to try to achieve this strategic goal. (We will talk more about intermediate and immediate tactical goals in the next few chapters, so do not worry about those just yet.)

THINK ABOUT HOW YOU WILL MEASURE PROGRESS TOWARD YOUR VISION

After you have figured out what your vision is, expressed in terms of customer outcomes that you want to help your customers achieve, you still usually have the problem of how you will measure whether you have achieved the goal. If you want to close a satisfaction gap, how will you know if you have achieved it?

Let us consider the goal of helping people learn anywhere they are, whenever they have available time. We might measure this through greater engagement, with more people engaging in learning activities at all hours of the day across the globe. This might tell us a lot, but we also want to make sure that they are getting what they want out of the learning activities. Therefore, we would want to measure their satisfaction with their experience and whether they can demonstrate that they have improved with the subject.

Thinking about measurement brings us to an even better formulation of the goal: to acquire knowledge and proficiency, from anywhere, at any time. The "better" goal earlier was still focused on the activity of learning, not the real goal that a person has in pursuing learning. No one wants to attend a class; what they want is to learn and improve their practice or proficiency at something. Even the class is simply a means to an end.

So, with this better goal, we need to ask how we can measure that improvement in proficiency and use those measures to determine if we are helping customers achieve their goals.

WHAT TO WATCH FOR

Organizations often define their goals by the things they want to achieve. Doing so is common, comfortable, and safe, but it is ambiguous and uninspired, and it is not very helpful when the organization needs to make strategic decisions. Organizations can create better strategic goals once they can articulate the needs and satisfaction gaps of their current and potential customers. This is measured through Unrealized Value, which EBM defines as "the potential future value that could be realized if the organization met the needs of all potential customers or users."

Another pitfall is when organizations gauge their success and progress through activity and output. These measurements are often used to reward people when they achieve them and to punish them when they do not. Weaponizing activities and output as performance goals make it almost impossible to learn anything, and it produces counterproductive behaviors like gaming measures and shifting blame.

Without outcome-driven goals that are purposefully centered on the customer and their needs, an organization is flying blindly while chasing cash and competitive advantages. In this chapter, we saw how Alpha invested millions of dollars in updating an internal process by building a new system that was well-intentioned but did not improve the customer experience. Alpha's goal was concentrated on what it thought was good for the company, not its customers, who were still struggling to receive quotes quickly. Customers were ultimately motivated to take their business elsewhere by Alpha's expensive yet weak initiative.

Organizations tend to favor goals centered on *outputs*, which are the things people produce, or *activities*, which are the things that people do, because they are easier to formulate and measure. These types of goals can misdirect the organization and employees from the true needs of their customers. They also hinder an organization from engaging and retaining creative and motivated employees who are invested in the experience of their customers and the organization's future.

MOVING FORWARD

Conversations around finding purpose can be quite difficult. You may be treading into waters that put jobs on the line or are nudging higher-level executives in a way they had not been nudged before. That does not mean you should avoid these conversations.

Consider a strategic goal to be the tree trunk of everything an organization does. Every branch and leaf relates to that trunk. All goals and measurements are influenced by it. If the trunk is rotting on the inside, you might not notice until it is too late.

Start by understanding what your current strategic goal is. Ask the questions around "why" against that goal. Think about outcomes, and drive to redesign the goal for the customer. Have transparent conversations about your goals and how you can improve them.

In this chapter, we have looked at how organizations must find purpose by looking through the eyes of their customers, why strategic goals should be focused on improving customer outcomes, and how measurement provides the feedback that organizations need to adapt their goals and strategies based on feedback. Even higher-level goals may change, and we want to know about those changes as early as possible. Next, we will look at how we can leverage empiricism to move toward those goals.

USING EMPIRICISM TO PROGRESS TOWARD GOALS

Be-Well, a healthcare provider, had a strategic goal:

To enable customers to quickly find a provider, schedule appointments, and communicate with their provider from any web browser or mobile device, at any time that is convenient for them.

Be-Well believed providing customers with easier access to healthcare services, better than any competitor in the market, would result in significant growth in new customers. They organized a program around achieving this goal whose motto, "Put the power of healthcare into patient hands," was evident in posters and marketing materials across the organization.

This program had a significant number of internal people with a vested interest in the program, including:

- Call center agents who would field customer inquiries
- Sales representatives selling the system to current and prospective customers
- Support staff, whose jobs would change with access to new data
- Executives who were funding the product

Managing these groups of people and their thoughts and opinions was the biggest challenge for the program. The program's management team implemented an internal management ecosystem to get feedback from these vested groups of people. That ecosystem included frequent meetings (daily, weekly, monthly) augmented by a digital dashboard that displayed the real-time status of important program measures.

As the program progressed, the dashboard showed what seemed like great progress. Productivity metrics showed that teams were getting progressively more efficient, and more and more features were being worked on. The dashboard displayed many different metrics, but these were the big four that executives and management fixated on as pillars of success:

1. **Program velocity:** The number of work items completed per timeframe. In this case, the timeframe was two weeks. This was interpreted as the business value that was being delivered every two weeks.

2. **Estimated versus actual:** When teams planned, how much of the planned work items were completed versus incomplete? These teams planned every two weeks. This was interpreted as a sign of the predictability of the program.

3. **Feature completion percentage:** For every key feature being worked on, the amount of remaining work was compared to the amount of completed work. This was interpreted as how close a team was to delivering a key capability.

4. **Retrospective commitment completion:** At the end of each planning cycle, teams were to meet and discuss improvement items they would work on in the next planning cycle. Those improvements were to be recorded and marked as complete or incomplete at the end of every cycle. A resulting completion percentage was calculated for the dashboard and interpreted as a sign of improved efficiency.

Everyone internally seemed happy with the program's progress. Everyone, that is, except customers. While teams had been working hard and delivering what they were told to deliver, feedback showed that customers were dissatisfied with the result. The call center was overloaded with complaints of a poorly designed user interface and missing functionality. Many customers remarked that they were better off following the old process of getting their healthcare. Web portal traffic started to dive. However, the program dashboards showed that lots of work was getting done, implying that customers were getting value, but in reality, they were missing the mark.

Teams can be busy delivering new features, and their customers can still be unhappy. Even with an outcome-oriented strategic goal, without intermediate and immediate tactical goals, an organization may lose sight of the value it is trying to deliver to the customer.

UNDERSTANDING VALUE

A surprising number of organizations never measure the value of what they deliver to customers. They focus on speed, efficiency, and controlling cost, but they ignore the people to whom they most need to listen. They figure that as long as customers buy or use their product, they must deliver something valuable. And when they release new versions of a product, as long as customers keep buying it, the new things in that release must have been valuable, too.

The reality is far more complex. Customers buy products for different reasons. They may hate the product but they have no alternative. They may find some parts of the product useful and never use others. Customers may love a particular product, find something that better meets their needs, and discard the old one.

Companies that do not measure the value they deliver may be wasting their time and money improving parts of their products that customers never use and do not care about. Meanwhile, they may be ignoring things that customers *do* care about. A company that does not measure the value it delivers to its customers simply flies blind, hoping that its guesses and preconceptions lead to business success. It needs to do better before someone else does.

Consider our Be-Well example for a moment. Armed with an outcome-oriented strategic goal, teams were busy delivering new customer capabilities. As long as they regarded success as merely delivering new capabilities, they assumed their work was valuable. Once they started measuring customer satisfaction, they realized that what they delivered was not what the customers wanted or needed.

When we introduced the strategic goal concept in Chapter 1, "Finding Purpose," we also introduced the concept of a *satisfaction gap*—or the difference between a customer's current experience and a customer's desired experience. The current experience in evidence-based management (EBM) is called *current value*.

Current Value (CV): The value delivered by the product today.

As with strategic goals, the best way to express CV is through outcomes that the customer experiences and finds valuable. Measuring CV and Unrealized Value (UV) at the same time helps teams and their organizations know whether they are progressing toward their strategic goals. The absolute value of CV and UV is unimportant; it is the size of the satisfaction gap (the difference between the customer's current experience and their desired experience) that matters.

To understand what outcomes customers may find valuable, you need to talk to them. Here are a few ways to talk with your customers:

- **Interviews:** Sit down with customers and ask them questions about your product. What is missing? What do they like? What do they not like? How does it help them?

- **Customer feedback groups:** Form concentrated groups of customers to have interactive conversations about the product. It is important to identify different customer types and ensure all are represented.

- **Online discussions:** There are so many online tools that you can leverage to interact with customers. Forums (and the like) are a great way to source information about customer needs and desires.

- **Watch them use your product:** With customer consent, you can look at what they do with your product and how they use it to accomplish something valuable to them. It is remarkable what you will see when you watch customers use your product.

Doing any of these might give you a better understanding of customers' satisfaction gap. You may uncover things they need to do to achieve the goals that your product does not help them with currently.

Customer satisfaction surveys may help to a limited extent to gauge general satisfaction, but they are rarely detailed enough to tell you much about how you can improve your product. Measures like Net Promoter Score (NPS) are so broad and unspecific that they are almost useless in understanding value.

The Blackberry is a cautionary tale and, unfortunately for them, a great example of a company not understanding Unrealized Value while Current Value looked great. People loved their Blackberry phones so much that, in 2009, President Barack Obama fought hard to keep his beloved Blackberry phone despite security concerns. And yet, just a few years later, Blackberry sales were dropping because consumer preferences had shifted toward iPhones and away from Blackberry's iconic QWERTY keyboard. A decade later, the Blackberry service was finally discontinued. What changed? Blackberry's Current Value had remained constant, but the satisfaction gap experienced by its customers had expanded.

PROGRESSING TOWARD GOALS IN A SERIES OF SMALL STEPS

Be-Well continued to work on improving its ability to reach its strategic goal by delivering releases of new portal capabilities to its customers. The feedback the company obtained was surprising. Some of the features it thought would help customers did not improve customer satisfaction. Furthermore, some features made things worse for the customer. Although the teams delivered features, progress toward their strategic goal seemed random, and the teams did not feel aligned. They felt that they were working hard but not making progress.

In some ways, getting feedback made the teams even more confused about what they needed to do next. Some internal voices, convinced of the value of certain features, questioned the validity of the data. Developers, accustomed to trusting what the internal voices of stakeholders said, now questioned the feedback that certain people within the organization were providing. Features that seemed valuable to internal voices—especially the loudest—seemed to have little value to customers. After six months of delivering new capabilities and measuring the result, the organization felt no closer to its strategic goal than when it began.

The challenges experienced by Be-Well are common. Organizations with only strategic goals often struggle to effectively manage their day-to-day work. They need something more near-term to help them focus. They also need to ensure that achieving those near-term goals leads them toward longer-term goals.

As mentioned in the Introduction, Evidence-Based Management uses three types of goals: strategic, intermediate, and immediate tactical. We have already discussed strategic goals. As Be-Well has discovered, strategic goals are important but insufficient because they are too far into the future to guide current decisions. For this, we use two additional types of shorter-term goals:

- *Intermediate goals* are achievements that will indicate that the organization is on the path to its strategic goal. The path to the intermediate goal is often still somewhat uncertain but not completely unknown. To take smaller, focused steps toward strategic and intermediate goals, organizations also need intermediate tactical goals.
- *Immediate tactical goals* are critical near-term objectives toward which an individual, team, or group of teams can work over a short period of time, ranging from a few weeks to a month.

Breaking big goals into a series of short-term goals is important because achieving each short-term goal provides a team with new information. That new information helps them understand what next step they might need to take to make progress toward the next-level goal. This is what we mean by the term *empiricism*. Simply put, empiricism is an approach in which all learning comes from experience.

Empiricism: The theory that all knowledge is derived from sense-experience.[1]

The situation at Be-Well in the opening story of this chapter illustrates why it is not enough to have strategic goals. Strategic goals are simply too far off and too ambitious to help teams focus their daily work. They need something more immediately achievable to guide them. At the same time, immediate tactical goals are too short-term in their focus to help teams work toward their strategic goal. Intermediate goals help teams connect their work to achieve immediate tactical goals with their long-term strategic goals.

---

1. The definition of empiricism cited from https://languages.oup.com/google-dictionary-en/

TAKING SMALL STEPS TOWARD GOALS

To achieve goals, organizations need to learn how to try new ideas in a deliberate and focused way. The three different levels of goals in EBM—from short-term (immediate tactical) to near-term (immediate) to long-term (strategic)—provide focus at varying levels. This is illustrated in the experiment loop (see Figure 2.1). The experiment loop helps teams and their organizations move from their current state toward their next immediate tactical goal while aligning with the strategic goal.

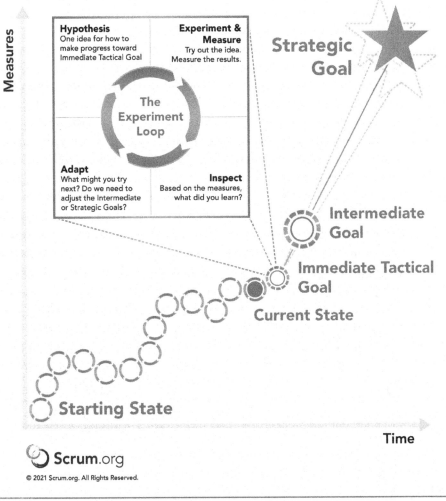

Figure 2.1 The experiment loop helps organizations move toward goals.

This experiment loop helps teams and their organizations move from their current state toward their next immediate tactical goal. Achieving immediate tactical goals helps them achieve their intermediate goals, which in turn helps them achieve their strategic goal.

In EBM, we work toward strategic goals by taking small, measured steps. Each step is an explicit hypothesis. Using explicit hypotheses is necessary when the path to achieving goals is uncertain. It helps teams try different ideas and approaches without over-investing in an idea that may not deliver the desired result.

This loop consists of the following:

- **Forming a hypothesis for improvement:** To plot their course toward their next intermediate goal, people and teams formulate ideas on what they need to achieve to take steps toward achieving that intermediate goal. Those steps are their immediate tactical goal. They then discuss ideas of things they think they can do to help them achieve their immediate tactical goal. They do not know whether doing these things will help them achieve their short-term goal, but they hypothesize that they will. Their immediate tactical goal needs to be measurable so that they will know whether they have achieved it, such as having evidence that they have delivered the customer outcome that they set out to deliver. To avoid experiments running forever, we recommend that teams work in defined timeboxes.

- **Running experiments:** The team members then work against the plan they have created to achieve their immediate tactical goal. They may adapt their plan as they learn things and acquire new information. Those adaptations help them achieve their immediate tactical goal. If their immediate tactical goal focuses on improving customer experiences, as most should, they need to deliver new capabilities to customers and measure the result.

- **Inspecting results:** At the end of the defined timebox for improvement, the team members assess whether they achieved their immediate tactical goal, as defined by the measurement targets they achieved.

- **Adapting goals or approaches based on what was learned:** If the team members achieve their immediate tactical goal, their next experiment loop will focus on forming a new immediate tactical goal that they think will take them closer to achieving their intermediate goal. If the team did not achieve its immediate tactical goal, it needs to ask whether a lack of understanding caused the shortfall or if their plans didn't have the desired outcome. The answers to these questions will help them improve in the next experiment loop.

One more thing teams need to consider is whether the goals are still correct. As we step toward goals, teams may have learned something that helps them form better goals. For instance, when teams find out what they think customers need is different from what customers need, the team must refine its goals accordingly. Likewise, they may have found that something in the market has shifted, and customers no longer have the same needs. These learnings may affect goals at every level: immediate tactical, intermediate, and even strategic.

Imagine being a video game company in the early 1980s with the goal of producing a market-differentiating arcade game. At the time, the market, was saturated, which led to a temporary crash of the industry, putting many video game development companies out of business. Others adapted their goals to meet growing customer demands for new and better systems. Those companies ended up producing iconic retro games still beloved today. If those companies had not constantly questioned their goals from a consumer standpoint, we would not know those titles today.

Adapting goals in the face of new information is important as long as it is not simply "moving the goalpost" to make it easier for teams or the organization to declare false victory.

Why Experiment?

In short, you experiment because you cannot know what is valuable and what is not. Even when you know something is valuable, you may find it difficult to design, build, and deliver that valuable capability to your customers.

The reality is that most of what people think they know is just unsubstantiated belief. Turning to "experts" is not much help either because they suffer from the same biases. They may know a lot about what has worked in the past, but their decisions involve guessing what will work in the future. That is where experimentation helps.

We have encountered managers who think experimentation is wasteful. They think, "Why should we build something that we do not know is valuable?" The problem is that, in a complex world, we cannot know what customers will find valuable. What is *really* wasteful is investing lots of money and time building something you think is valuable, only to find that it is not. We have seen that time and again.

The term *experiment* may be a stumbling block for some. They may believe it means merely trying random things and hoping for the best. We mean something very different. Experiments involve forming a specific hypothesis, which is a statement you think is true, but experiments also involve defining how you will know if that hypothesis is false.

Experimentation is a way to learn. It is a way of narrowing alternatives and rejecting ideas that do not lead you toward the goals you are trying to reach. It is the opposite of "just doing things and seeing how they work out." It takes time and practice to master, but it is the only way to progress toward ambitious goals in an uncertain, complex world.

STEERING TOWARD GOALS

Organizations that are steeped in traditional planning approaches might feel that the best way to reach a goal is to establish a plan for reaching that goal and then execute that plan. If the world were completely certain—if organizations could create plans that could foresee every possibility—they might succeed. Unfortunately, as we all know, the world is quite uncertain.

Imagine the planning sessions in 2019 for the year 2020 for major pharmaceutical companies such as Johnson & Johnson and Pfizer. As 2020 began, the execution of the plans began. Then the COVID-19 pandemic struck and changed everything for them. Those companies pivoted on a dime, with the sole intention of creating a vaccine. All hands were on deck as major strategic initiatives shifted. What if they had just stuck to the original plans they created in 2019? Again, the world is quite uncertain.

As Figure 2.1 implies, strategic goals, spanning many years, are so far off that it is impossible to make plans to reach them. Even intermediate goals, spanning 3–6 months, are almost impossible to achieve with a single, simple plan. Only immediate tactical goals, which are the most short-term, are realistically achievable in a single pass. Achieving a series of thoughtfully created immediate tactical goals can lead a team to achieve a series of intermediate goals that eventually lead to achieving a strategic goal.

If you look carefully at Figure 2.1, you see that the path to achieving an intermediate goal is not a straight line. There is quite a bit of uncertainty on our journey to accomplishing an intermediate goal. We cope with that uncertainty with immediate tactical goals. The information we learn when executing an immediate tactical goal helps us define the next. This is why planning a series of immediate tactical goals far in advance is a mistake. The uncertainty that exists with strategic goals is even greater. Goals change because the organization learns things by running experiments that help them refine and reformulate the goals.

As teams run experiments and an organization considers how teams are progressing toward their goals, they should continually ask themselves these questions:

• Are we making progress toward our goals?
• Are those goals the right goals for what we want to achieve?

The experiment loop provides the mechanism for teams and their organizations to gather the information to answer these questions. When organizations try to solve complex problems, their path is always uncertain.

ADAPTING GOALS

Ole' Foam Brewery was a small craft brewer operated out of Milwaukee, Wisconsin, with the slogan "carefully delicious brewed beer." Their flagship beer, Peace Foam, had a stellar reputation as a high-quality pilsner. Their CEO, Lex, had big dreams for the company, and he shared his strategic goal to "have the market-leading beer in the USA." Lex intended to make Peace Foam that beer.

To grow market share, Lex pressured the brewmasters and production managers to increase the output of Peace Foam as their first intermediate goal to get the beer into more customers' hands. In response, the brewers and production manager reduced the brewing process from forty-five to fifteen days per batch of Peace Foam. To achieve this, they had to change one of the major ingredients of Peace Foam.

This shortened brew cycle continued for several months. Then several brew assistants reported that the taste was not quite the same as the Peace Foam everyone had come to love. Lex sampled the product himself but shrugged off the feedback, saying that it tasted close enough to him.

The organization appeared to have met its intermediate goal: increasing production by 300 percent in six months. Lex made deals in different states and began the broader marketing and distribution of Peace Foam. He felt confident that the organization was well on its way to achieving its strategic goal to "have the market-leading beer in the USA."

As distribution progressed, Lex started receiving phone calls from unhappy customers returning the beer to distribution centers because of the taste. They reported that the taste was so bad that it was undrinkable. In the end, Ole' Foam Brewery ended up recalling all the beer it had distributed. It had followed the plan and was successfully scaling production, but its reputation was spoiled by the incident, and it never fully recovered. A competitor eventually bought Ole' Foam Brewery, and today, the brewer is but a footnote in the industry's history.

Plan-driven organizations usually have small executive teams developing plans that the rest of the organization then dutifully follows. The organization usually assumes that any failures of the teams to produce the expected results are due to the teams not following the plan rather than the plan itself being wrong.

Teams may fail because they do not follow the plan. Still, it has been our experience that the case of Ole' Foam Brewery is more typical than a lot of executives would like to admit. Their plans fail because they are based on flawed assumptions. In the case of Ole' Foam Brewery, the assumption was that production times could be dramatically cut without reducing quality.

Assumptions like this can be wrong, but they can also be right. There is no way to know without experimenting. The problem Ole' Foam Brewery and similar companies make is not trying things but committing to that decision without validating the decision with actual data. Strong executives are praised for their unwavering belief, but if their beliefs are wrong, they can take the company down with them.

Instead of plunging ahead based on untested assumptions, what if Ole' Foam Brewery had experimented with different ways to increase volume without cutting quality? Most of their experiments might fail, but it is better to get earlier feedback and try other alternatives than to commit everything to an unexamined approach.

When working in an outcome-oriented, goal-driven approach like EBM, people's attention moves from following a plan to achieving a desired result. When teams fail to achieve the desired result, they should ask themselves whether they learned anything that told them the goal needs to be changed or improved.

Goals can change because of outside events, and you may need to reconsider and revise your tactics to reach your goals. Was the intermediate goal the right goal? Is the strategic goal still relevant? If you achieve the intermediate goal, you need to choose a new intermediate goal. If you did not achieve it, you must decide whether you need to persevere, stop, or pivot toward something new. If your strategic goal is no longer relevant, you need to either adapt it or replace it.

Important conversations also arise when teams learn something new, especially when people learn things that make them reconsider goals. Goals are never perfect, and they need to be adapted just as much as tactics. Goals may be too aspirational to be achievable, or they may not stretch teams or organizations enough to be motivating and inspiring. They may also be just plain wrong, as when they assume that customers need one thing, but they in fact need something different.

ADAPTING TACTICS

Once team members confirm that their goals are still the right ones, they need to consider how they can work better to achieve those goals. They might need to reduce interruptions, obtain the expertise they lack, improve their focus, or even reduce the scope of their immediate tactical goal, not to take on more work than they can reasonably complete in their improvement timebox. Improving focus bears special attention; teams can work incredibly hard on too many things and, as a result, fail to meet their goals.

Whatever their findings, teams use their reflections to improve their next experiment loop. We will cover this topic extensively in the next and leave further discussion until then.

THE REAL PURPOSE OF GOALS IS TO FOSTER CONVERSATIONS

Some managers use goals in a rather clumsy carrot-and-stick approach that they think will motivate employees. For them, goals are generated top-down, and it is up to the teams to meet their assigned goals and achieve their rewards, or they fail to meet the goals and suffer the consequences. In reality, goals are guesses and need to be refined based on feedback just as much as a team's tactics to reach a goal. This is just as true for strategic and intermediate goals as for immediate tactical goals.

Goal setting is an opportunity for collaboration and alignment around important goals. It is a chance to discuss, refine, and sometimes refocus based on feedback. In a complex world, engaging everyone in seeking better goals using feedback to inspect and adapt helps organizations improve the quality and value of the outcomes they provide to their customers.

Although senior leadership tends to set strategic goals, even these goals benefit from conversations with team members, who often have important insights into customer needs and satisfaction gaps.

Intermediate goals are at the intersection between strategic vision and tactical execution, and they benefit most from active conversations between executives and team members. These conversations tend to focus on how achieving an intermediate goal will indicate progress toward the strategic goal and what measures will show that the intermediate goal has been achieved.

Immediate tactical goals mostly stimulate conversations within teams because team members ask themselves what they need to achieve or what they need to learn to feel confident that they are making progress toward their next intermediate goal.

LOSING THE PLOT AND FINDING IT AGAIN

Long-running programs can take on a life of their own, losing sight of what they originally set out to achieve. The experience of a large insurance company quoting system program illustrates the point.

Several years into the program, Ensure-You had five teams busily working on features, yet no one understood who needed them and why. Many were focused on meeting internal reporting needs and making the work easier, but the program had no proof that the quoting process was improving. Program milestones were always met, but some people in the organization felt that the program was off track.

After some digging, they rediscovered documents that described the original program goals, including the customer satisfaction gap they wanted to close. The program goal was to make it far easier for customers to get quote information through a self-service portal, reducing the time from ten days to one.

Several years and millions of dollars later, customer quote time had not improved, and customers were no more capable of getting the information they needed. This was a goal still worth centering the program around. They realized the problem was that the organization had no intermediate goals, only immediate tactical goals and a strategic goal. There was too much disconnect.

To remedy this, Ensure-You put in place an intermediate goal to reduce the time it takes for a customer to obtain a quote. The initial intermediate goal was set to reduce the time it took customers to receive a quote by 50% (down to five days) in the next six months. Reminding everyone of the strategic goal and establishing an intermediate goal helped everyone focus and align. The program started to improve.

Large multi-year programs tend to take on a life of their own, losing sight of what they originally set out to achieve. Once programs are funded, people in the organization can see them as opportunities to fulfill long-standing perceived needs or get things "fixed" that they feel have been long neglected. These things are important to stakeholders but may not help the organization achieve its goals.

Without effective intermediate goals, it is easy for people working on these programs to lose sight of the program goal and, on the other hand, for management to question why teams are working on those things. Even when teams meet their immediate tactical goals, their work can drift from helping to achieve the strategic goal because their immediate tactical goals have become disconnected from the strategic goal. Effective intermediate goals help to solve this problem.

WHAT TO WATCH FOR

The beginning of this chapter started with the story of Be-Well, a company that created an outcome-based strategic goal that quickly lost sight of the customer. Instead of customer dialogue and focusing on satisfied customers, Be-Well defined, as organizations often do, their success by how efficiently teams were getting work done. And they did that well because they were very busy. Teams collaborated and delivered features quickly. But in the end, customers get the final say in what they feel is valuable for them. A company's customers define the satisfaction gap. Believing otherwise is burying your head in the sand and refusing reality. That is why EBM uses three levels of goals (strategic, intermediate, and immediate tactical) to understand progress.

As you start to form or reform goals with your team and organization, remember that these goals are not carved in stone and will not always be correct—especially strategic goals. Organizations should regard their goals as fluid, evolving as information, situations, and priorities change. This is another reason fixed plans in an agile environment fail: They are based on outdated information.

MOVING FORWARD

In Chapter 1, we compared the strategic goal to a tree trunk. Intermediate goals are the limbs connected to that trunk, and immediate tactical goals are like branches off each limb. As in nature, where there is seldom a straight trunk, limb, or branch, there is never a straight and linear path toward a strategic goal.

It takes many intermediate goals to get close to reaching a strategic goal. The same can be said for intermediate goals and how we take even smaller steps to achieve them with immediate tactical goals. At the foundation of Evidence-Based Management is empiricism, so people can use empiricism to progressively achieve and learn about their goals, one step at a time.

How will you know that an immediate tactical goal has helped you take a step toward the intermediate goal? And how will you know that an intermediate goal is getting you closer to the strategic goal? Use measurement and focus on CV to answer these questions, especially when an organization struggles to define and align goals. Look for the benefit to the customers. How do you know this information to be true? Remember to get out and talk to your customers.

In this chapter, we emphasized the need to understand the value you are delivering to customers, how to progress using the different levels of goals (immediate tactical, intermediate, and strategic), and how to leverage empiricism as you take steps toward each level of goal by defining experiments and measurements that will allow you to learn whether those needs and desires were warranted. The true purpose of all of these ideas is to have better conversations. In the next chapter, we will discuss what it takes to become more effective.

BECOMING (MORE) EFFECTIVE

EatUp had been producing a restaurant solution to handle everything from front-of-house point of sale to inventory management for many years. Unfortunately, the company's comprehensive, robust product was becoming old and outdated. Its largest competitor was taking some of its market share with a more modern user interface and a system that was much easier to use.

To keep up with the competition, EatUp strategically focused 80 percent of its finances on a complete rewrite of its product, making it like new. After two years, the company had a bare-bones solution ready to deliver to its customers. But even then, the solution was far behind what its competitors offered and missed key features customers desired.

While EatUp was stuck between maintaining support for its existing application and getting customers to migrate to the new version, its competitor kept getting further ahead. EatUp was about to go out of business if it couldn't find a solution. Customers were leaving in droves.

EatUp's case is a familiar one. A company that once was an industry leader was quickly finding itself behind a competitor because of legacy technology. The company addressed the satisfaction gap too late and responded by trying to rewrite an existing application from the ground up. EatUp thought the rewrite would improve its ability to deliver competitive new technology to customers quickly and effectively. In reality, its approach never paid off and further limited its agility.

Agility can help organizations deliver more rapidly, but that is not its real purpose. And it is not just about getting better at responding to change. Any organization merely responding to change is letting its reality be defined by someone else. Agility helps organizations turn their ability to respond to new information into a competitive advantage. It is not just about changing the products and services a company delivers to customers; agility is also about adapting the company's goals to new market realities.

Companies must balance being fast with being effective. When considering that balance, they must not lose sight of their customers and the value they bring (or could bring) to them. We will dig into this further.

VALUE IS ESSENTIAL, BUT FREQUENCY MATTERS TOO

If an organization or team cannot deliver potential improvements in current value (CV) in rapid succession, it cannot obtain feedback from customers and cannot respond quickly to that feedback. Relative to the value the product delivers, it is flying blind and unable to see problems until it is too late to address them.

To improve value delivery, an organization and its teams first need to improve their ability to deliver value. If they don't, they may risk suffering the same fate as EatUp, which could not deliver effectively because old technology was not addressed in a timely manner. When EatUp finally decided to update their technology, they started over and spent two years rewriting everything from scratch. No one should be surprised that by the time they were ready to deliver two years later, the market dynamics had changed, pushing them even further behind in learning about what their customers wanted—the satisfaction gap—and delivering those capabilities to.

Most organizations have a sizable satisfaction gap, although they may not know it until they start measuring. Having a large satisfaction gap, measured by unrealized value (UV), may not sound like a good thing at first, but it is. It means the organization has a large opportunity to create customer value. Organizations with a small satisfaction gap have fewer opportunities to improve customer experiences and, therefore, fewer opportunities for growth.

Most organizations with a large satisfaction gap cannot quickly close it, meaning they have a limited ability to create value. Because it takes so long for them to deliver anything to customers that *might* be valuable, they lose sight of their goals. They are not even sure what things they should be working on today, never mind how to be competitive in the future. They feel lost and like they never make progress toward their goals.

Organizations in this situation usually recognize it, and their immediate reaction is to focus on "going faster," which means delivering more frequently. In evidence-based management (EBM) terms, they focus on reducing their Time to Market (T2M).

Time to Market (T2M): The organization's ability to quickly deliver new capabilities, services, or products.

Examples of things organizations can measure to understand their T2M include:

- **Customer cycle time:** The amount of time between when work starts and when it is released to the customer. This measure reflects an organization's ability to reach its customer.

- **Lead time:** The amount of time between when an idea is proposed or a hypothesis is formed and when a customer can benefit from that idea. This measure may vary based on the customer and product. It is a contributing factor to customer satisfaction.

- **Time to learn:** The total time needed to come up with or sketch an idea for improvement, build it, deliver it to users, and learn from its usage.

- **Time to pivot:** A measure of true business agility that presents the elapsed time between when an organization receives feedback or new information and when it responds to that feedback. For example, it might be the time between when an organization finds out a competitor has delivered a new market-winning feature and when the organization responds with new matching or exceeding capabilities that measurably improve customer experience.

Shortening T2M is important for organizations seeking to be more responsive to customer needs, and it is frequently the first place organizations start when seeking to improve their ability to deliver. Following are some examples of what organizations can do to improve their T2M[1]:

- Simplifying workflows and reducing hand-offs between teams and people
- Automating repetitive tasks
- Reducing waste resulting from too much work in progress (WIP)
- Reducing the scope of releases

IT IS NOT DELIVERY SPEED THAT IS IMPORTANT; IT IS FEEDBACK SPEED

We have worked with many organizations for whom speedy delivery has become their primary goal. These organizations usually assume they know what customers find valuable, and they just need to deliver it faster. Yet ample data from leading organizations indicates ideas about what customers find valuable are often wrong.[2]

Some managers are obsessed with speed because they think of the organization as a factory line that produces earnings. They believe the faster they can run the production line, the more money the organization will make. This perspective is too simplistic for complex work, and it is wrong. In a changing world, going fast without being able to change direction means you can get off-track even faster. Ultimately, speed is important because you obtain critical information that you need to change direction faster.

---

1. This is not an exhaustive list of things an organization can do to improve its T2M. We will discuss specific improvement strategies in more depth in subsequent chapters.
2. For more about why it is important to run experiments and measure value, see www.infoq.com/articles/empiricism-business-agility/?itm_source=infoq&itm_campaign=user_page&itm_medium=link.

The primary reason to improve T2M is not to "go faster." It is to get better information faster about what customers need. Faster delivery means more frequent and relevant customer feedback. Measuring "speed" implies one-way delivery. When organizations do that, they ignore the possibility that their actions might not be valuable.

Once an organization can deliver a new capability frequently (perhaps monthly), it can measure value often enough to get a better sense of what is valuable. For digital products, however, most organizations need to get their T2M down to days, not weeks, to run effective experiments about value.

WHILE FOCUSING ON SPEED, DO NOT LOSE SIGHT OF VALUE

In the earlier days of the world's response to COVID-19, companies everywhere scrambled to respond to people's demand for information about avoiding exposure and communicate to their network if they were exposed when entering post-lockdown life. Contact tracking became a big thing.

One organization delivered a mobile app that allowed health authorities to capture information about who people had come in contact with simply by using location information gathered with their cell phones. By allowing the app to track them, people could learn if someone else (who also had enabled tracking) had come down with COVID-19, and the health authority could access people's contact details and decide whether people should test for the virus and quarantine.

The app was extremely easy to use and very popular. Unfortunately, it was hacked, resulting in a massive data leak and the unauthorized sharing of potentially private information. The risks outweighed the benefits for users, and they quickly abandoned the app, resulting in lost revenue for the company and also a loss of a valuable exposure information for epidemiology research. The organization that created the app also lost because it hoped to benefit from the data collection for future commercial purposes.

This situation illustrates an important point: Even when speed is critical, value is important. The users of the exposure-tracking app wanted a quick solution that would tell them about their possible exposure and exposure in their network of contacts, as illustrated by the rapid adoption of the app. At the same time, users most certainly *did not* want to sacrifice their privacy, as illustrated by their rapid departure from the app once the data breach became known.

Even your situation does not have such dire implications as a data breach it is easy to fall into the trap of focusing on speed while losing sight of value. The illusion is that speed will lead to value, but that is not always true.

SPEED IS NOT ENOUGH; TEAMS MUST ALSO BE EFFECTIVE

Although improving T2M is important, if each release closes the satisfaction gap just a tiny amount, the organization does not make fast progress toward its goal. Consider the following example.

> RightRx builds software to help pharmacies manage their operations by handling everything from detecting potential drug interactions to managing inventory. The company's major market differentiator is that it can stand up new pharmacies with custom-tailored solutions faster than any competitor and at a lower cost.
>
> However, the very ease of customization that had differentiated RightRx from its competitors was preventing customers from upgrading to newer versions of the base product. In essence, every customer was running a slightly different version of the software.
>
> Without a way to bring these customizations to a new version, customers refused to upgrade. Maintaining all these different customer versions of their product was becoming expensive, and the unwillingness of customers to upgrade limited RightRx's long-term revenue potential.

Although RightRx was able to get a new customer up and running quickly, the company's long-term effectiveness was limited due to the many versions it needed to support across different customers. Over time, CV for RightRx declined because customers wanted features that RightRx could not deliver effectively. They were also limited in their capacity to gain new UV because their skill in closing satisfaction gaps by introducing new products was immature. In EBM terms, RightRx was limited in its Ability to Innovate (A2I).

Ability to Innovate (A2I): The effectiveness of an organization to deliver new capabilities that might better meet customer needs.

Measuring A2I tells organizations how impactful their work is. Examples of things organizations can measure to understand their A2I include the following:

- **Average daily interruptions:** The average number of times team members are interrupted during the day.

- **Innovation rate:** The percentage of effort or cost spent on new product capabilities is divided by the total product effort or cost. This provides insight into the capacity of the organization to deliver new product capabilities.

- **On-product index:** The percentage of time teams spend working on product and value.

- **Installed version index:** The number currently supported product versions.

Organizations can do some things to improve their A2I[3]:

- Reduce interruptions, distractions, and diversions that prevent them from focusing on value-added product work, such as handling production incidents, working on other products or projects, or attending non-product related meetings

- Eliminate waste that results from undone work

- Eliminate rework caused by accepting poor quality work or deferring decisions

---

3. This is not an exhaustive list of things an organization can do to improve its T2M. We will discuss specific improvement strategies in more depth in subsequent chapters.

These improvements may also improve T2M by reducing interruptions and letting the team focus. To gain a complete picture of a team's delivery capability, a team must also look at the impact on Current Value (CV) a release. Measuring the change in CV resulting from a release is ultimately most important, but the time it takes to measure CV and the large number of factors that affect it can obscure easy-to-spot improvements.

RightRx's tracking of the installed version index helped the company realize that having too many software versions in customer's hands reduced its effectiveness by imposing a kind of "update tax." Every time the company needed to make a change, it had to update all the different product versions. Once RightRx understood how much that was affecting its A2I (and eventually, its CV), it invested time and money into making the system much easier to upgrade. In doing so, RightRx saved money, increased its T2M, and retained a happier customer base that could more quickly receive desired features.

TOO MANY THINGS AT ONCE

You are sitting next to a colleague, Maia, as you both work on creating a marketing brochure your boss would like to see a prototype of by the end of the week. Maia is on her laptop responding to emails while simultaneously jumping in and out of conversations with you. She suddenly gets up and leaves, scurrying to a meeting related to another project.

Two hours later, you and Maia reconvene. You show her what you did while she was gone. She thinks it is good progress but wants to make some adjustments. But, just then, your boss summons you into an urgent meeting to discuss a problem project that has gone on endlessly. You and Maia decide to finish the brochure the next day so you can focus on it without distractions. You have to stay late, but you ultimately finish it. You agree that it could have been better, but you did not have time to focus on it.

Does that kind of day sound familiar to you? Are you constantly shifting gears in and out of different contexts? To be effective, we need to focus. Focusing on more than one thing at a time is detrimental to our ability to complete anything. Figure 3.1[4] illustrates the loss of productivity due to context switching when working on multiple projects.

Task Switching

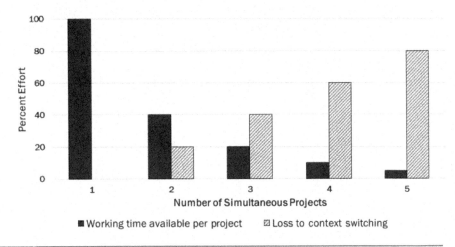

Figure 3.1 The cost of task switching.

As Figure 3.1 illustrates, context switching is expensive when considering how much we lose when working on multiple projects. To make this transparent, you can make a similar chart showing the number of employees on the vertical axis and the number of projects on the horizontal axis. Limiting the number of things employees work on simultaneously increases an organization's effectiveness. And yet, most organizations think keeping their employees busy, and working at their maximum capacities is the best way to maximize their investment in their workforce.

These same limiting work-in-progress rules apply at all levels, from the number of projects being worked on to the number of active goals. To get things done and optimize the ability and effectiveness of teams, we must limit the amount of work, so those teams can focus.

---

4. Figure 3.1 Source: Gerald Weinberg, Quality Software Management: Systems Thinking

WHERE SHOULD TEAMS START?

Teams can find it challenging to decide what they should focus on first. They will always be under pressure to deliver more product capabilities, but if they cannot measure the impact of what they deliver in rapid cycles, they run a high chance of producing features that do not help them improve their customer outcomes. Figure 3.2 shows a decision tree to assist in focusing their improvement efforts.

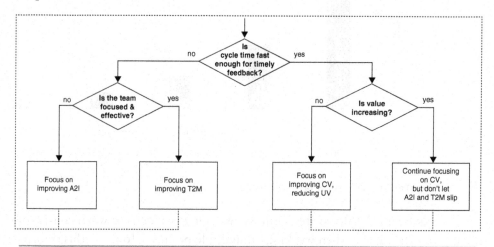

Figure 3.2 Where to focus depends on where the organization is today.

In this model, while value (increasing CV and reducing UV) is most important for reaching strategic goals, teams that cannot test new ideas quickly may find they are focusing on the wrong product capabilities. To improve their ability to deliver value, they may choose to focus on improving their A2I and T2M. We suggest focusing first on improving A2I because doing so improves the team's ability to focus on improving T2M and, ultimately, CV/UV.

As the team's A2I and T2M improve, they will be more effective at running experiments focused on improving the value they deliver because they will be better able to gather and act upon customer feedback. These experiments typically focus on trying potential solutions to better meet customer needs or gathering information that improves their understanding of the customer's desired outcomes and current satisfaction.

BEWARE THE EFFICIENCY TRAP

Organizations often focus on efficiency when they should focus on effectiveness. One reason is that they use the terms *efficiency* and *effectiveness* interchangeably when they are, in fact two very distinct concepts.

Efficiency refers to the ability to do something in a way that minimizes the use of resources, such as time, money, and effort. It is the measure of how well something is done. This factor may look at how much work is done, its quality, and how quickly it was finished.

Effectiveness refers to the extent to which something successfully achieves its intended goals. It measures how well something achieves its objectives.

For instance, a highly efficient team may deliver many product features promptly. Still, if those features are not valuable to the customer—and the team members are not adapting their work based on customer feedback—then although they may be efficient, they are also ineffective. The team may simply be good at delivering the wrong things quickly. Teams (and organizations) are effective when they can deliver value to customers collaboratively and sustainably.

If a team tries to become efficient before it becomes effective, it may simply reinforce ineffective working methods. Efficiency improvement initiatives may reduce cost, but they may also reduce the ability of the team to become effective by eliminating activities that might help identify what they really should be working on. The biggest source of waste for a team is building things that customers do not need.

Once a team is effective, it can shift to becoming more *efficient* by focusing on eliminating non-value-added activities that prevent the team from delivering quickly or delivering as much value as it can. Automation plays a role in this, but a larger role is usually played by frequent interruptions and being pulled away to work on things that do not add value.

One example of non-value-added work includes meetings to coordinate between teams, would not be needed if the delivery team members were sufficiently skilled to simply do the work themselves. Another example is having to seek approval from someone for a decision, would not be needed if the delivery team was sufficiently empowered.

BALANCING SPEED AND EFFECTIVENESS

As discussed, being effective is essential. And yet, teams must balance their efforts to become more effective with their ability to deliver quickly. If they do not deliver something to their customers, they cannot produce anything of value, nor can they test their assumptions about what is valuable.

We often encounter teams and organizations that spend considerable time and money trying to become more effective (usually focusing on aligned objectives) but are taking too long to deliver valuable product increments to their customers. This limits their ability to grow CV and decrease UV. Consider the following example:

> Purple Tangerine is a premier boutique design firm most widely known for its ability to create new brands for companies. At the center of the firm's success was a super team internally known as "the It Squad." The problem was that a single team had become a bottleneck for the entire organization. To increase T2M and A2I, the CEO decided to split the team and reorganize the company.
>
> After six months, the firm had become quite slow when responding to customers. For the first time in the company's history, existing customers were unhappy, and it became harder to acquire new customers. The re-org appeared not to be working, so the CEO decided to re-team. Yet, problems with existing customers only increased. Current value was dropping, and Purple Tangerine was less effective and slower than before. The CEO contemplated what to do next.

With Purple Tangerine in mind, consider the decision tree in Figure 3.2. Initially, at the top of the tree, they realized cycle time was not fast enough due to the limitations of a single team. That led the CEO to initiate the re-org to spread the It Squad members to other teams and areas, so they could share their process and practices with the rest of the organization.

The CEO thought the firm would deliver faster and be more effective by scaling and duplicating the processes that once made the It Squad successful.

Purple Tangerine became so focused on its internal processes that it neglected its existing customers. Even the team's goals were inward-looking, meaning they reflected the new team structure and process improvements instead of customers and value. They did not revisit the decision tree frequently to see if their situation had changed and did not inspect and adapt.

Keep an eye on situations where organizations and teams overly focus their improvement efforts on team collaboration or capability expansion and lose sight of their primary goal: delivering value to customers. Effectiveness is important, but so is speed. Teams need to achieve a balance between effectiveness, A2I, and speed, time to market.

CUTTING CORNERS: SOMETIMES NECESSARY, SOMETIMES FATAL

Teams often struggle to balance the desire to be absolutely perfect and wholly complete with the desire to get something useful but imperfect out the door so they can learn and improve later. Neither desire is wrong; both are necessary to get things done. However, unchecked perfectionism usually results in slow learning, and nothing ever getting done because nothing is ever perfect. At the same time, the line between "good enough" and "unsuitably shoddy" is easy to cross without being aware of it. Neither extreme helps customers.

The problem is that "good enough" is up to the customer, not the team, and the team has to deliver something to find out where that line is. Sometimes, shortcuts are necessary to get valuable feedback, but the team has to be careful to avoid creating a bigger problem for itself later on. Consider the following example:

> A major US air carrier had heard for years from employees that the processes and systems crew members used to reschedule their flights due to illness, weather, or aircraft mechanical problems were slow and ineffective,

even under the best of circumstances. During minor storms, crew members often had to call someone to manually handle the crew changes.

Major events created so much manual work that crew members had to wait on hold on the phone for hours to process the changes. These delays caused ripple effects that spread throughout the system. When delayed flights could not get the crews they needed, more flights were delayed, causing even more crew members to reschedule until the entire system would break down. The software often resulted in outages that caused the company to transition into a manual mode of communication for scheduling crew by phone.

When major delays happened at peak holiday travel, thousands of passengers were stranded, costing the airline an estimated $800 million in losses, a smeared reputation, and scarred customers who may never return.

The CEO and executives were long aware of the crew scheduling problem, but they continually postponed dealing with it to boost earnings and their bonuses.

At one time, airline's crew scheduling processes and systems were good enough, but growth in the number of flights and crews had strained the system to the breaking point, even under normal operations. The company had ignored signs that the system was no longer good enough and had failed to invest in finding a solution that would be good enough.

At the same time, we have seen countless situations in which an organization never actually released anything because it was constantly working on perfecting it. Eventually, the people paying the bills decided to cut the company's losses and stop these projects—but usually not before wasting millions of dollars and many years of effort.

Cutting corners and incurring debt may be necessary to lower unrealized value, increase current value or test ideas more quickly test that could lead to improvements in current value or reductions in unrealized value. But when you do this, you have to constantly evaluate whether the corner-cutting is not creating a larger problem that usually manifests itself in A2I as some sort of rework that will prevent a team or organization from being effective later because they are too busy dealing with a crisis. Had the US airline carrier thought about how the disruption would affect the A2I and the eventual detrimental impact on current value, it might have fixed the problem before it was too late.

WHAT TO WATCH FOR

Organizations often seek agility to improve their speed of delivery. Delivering solutions to customers more quickly, especially faster than competitors, is important to winning in the marketplace, though being fast is not enough. The solution must also be valuable to customers, and the only way to know is to measure changes in customer satisfaction.

We have encountered many companies in which decisions were largely based on internal suggestions, which can evolve into many of the examples we have shared in this chapter. Project sponsors and other internal voices can be valuable sources of ideas about improving customer value. Still, they are not customers, and customers are the final arbiters of value.

Although feedback is always valuable, it is not always pleasant. Sometimes, it is easier to ignore it in the latter case. However, an organization that thinks it deeply understands its customers and simply wants to "go faster" or "be more efficient" misses the humbling opportunity to learn when feedback points to a flawed strategy or products not meeting customers' needs.

T2M and A2I are easy and comfortable areas to focus on because progress and advancements are easy to measure. Do not fall for this bait. Always bring the conversations back to the value you could deliver to your existing and potential customers. Here are some other likely effects when an organization overemphasizes a single key value area (KVA):

- If they focus too much on current value without improving A2I, teams can experience burnout because no matter how hard they work, current value never seems to change very much.
- If they focus too much on current value without understanding unrealized value, they can waste a lot of effort trying to improve things that the

customer does not need to improve; what they have now is good enough, and the team and organization should focus on areas where customers have a satisfaction gap.

- If they focus too much on T2M or going faster without understanding CV and UV, they may simply be delivering things that customers do not care about. When people work hard but achieve very little, they also experience burnout.

MOVING FORWARD

Each KVA is like a lens that puts different things in focus. We use them together to help teams and organizations get a sense of where they should focus their improvement efforts. It is important to know that each KVA tends to affect the others:

- If A2I is poor—even if T2M is good—teams and organizations struggle to improve CV and reduce UV quickly because each release has only a small impact.
- If T2M is poor—even if A2I is good—teams and organizations struggle to improve current value and reduce unrealized value quickly because of the long time between releases.
- If CV remains poor and UV remains high over time—even when A2I and T2M are good—the team or organization does not understand their customers' satisfaction gaps (as measured by UV) well enough to deliver better experiences.

EBM's KVAs let organizations see what they need to improve and focus on so that they know if they are over-investing in one kind of improvement at the expense of others. They also provide information about the organization's capability and their teams' ability to deliver.

As we described, a team's ability to focus on improving customer experiences and to avoid interruptions, multitasking, and non-value-added meetings performs better than a team that focuses only on speed. Speed is important, but only if each release improves customer experiences and current value.

To rapidly improve current value, a team must have a fast T2M and high A2I. It must deliver in rapid cycles, but each release must also contain valuable capabilities that customers appreciate or at least thoughtful experiments about how the team can improve the current value of its product.

Think about your current situation. If you had to pick, which KVA are you most focused on? Is that creating an imbalance? Are you overlooking another KVA? What should you do next with that conclusion?

In this chapter, we looked at effectiveness, A2I, and speed, or T2M. Striking a balance in these areas allows an organization to more quickly test future value hypotheses. Overemphasizing in any area can cost you new or existing customers.

In the next chapter, we look at how we can use EBM to stimulate better conversations within a team and organization.

Managing and Overcoming Expectations

Bryan was a project manager for a large not-for-profit organization. Every Sunday evening, his anxiety increased as he started thinking about Tuesday's weekly project status meeting. Bryan was responsible for three different projects, each with its own problems. He felt that his project role was not so much "manager" as "chief firefighter."

Each project status meeting had Bryan reporting the summary status of his projects with simple color codes: green for "healthy," yellow for "challenged," and red for "troubled." Red projects tended to get a degree of executive scrutiny that no one found useful and threatened career advancement.

The truth, however, was that all of Bryan's projects were yellow at best. Bryan and his peers typically spent most of Monday accumulating data and producing charts that helped them make the case that their projects were green. Only in desperation would a project manager designate yellow, and no one ever reported red unless they were prepared to leave the company.

Bryan and the non-profit he worked for are not exceptions; we have worked with many organizations that use this approach to project status reporting. Most operate under the illusion that everything is working well, not having any clue that they have incentivized making a report look good over telling the truth.

For Evidenced-Based Management (EBM) to work, we need to break the habit of creating a mirage for the sake of making people happy. We can leverage goals and the four Key Value Areas (KVAs) to create better conversations sooner. We must guide our experiences while creating transparency about those experiences as we move forward. This enables an organization to make swifter decisions and live in reality rather than operating by the false pretense that everything is okay.

PEOPLE WHO LARGELY SEEK TO VALIDATE EXPECTATIONS ARE OFTEN DISAPPOINTED

Consider Bryan and the green-yellow-red reporting he was required to do for each of his projects. He frequently tried to rationalize ways to make his projects green when they were, in fact, yellow or red. Turning them yellow or red would have meant having upper management's eyes suddenly looking at the nuances of the projects.

People do not like surprises. They like to have their expectations met. They tend to look at data confirming their biases rather than data showing their expectations to be wrong. That is neither good nor bad; it is just human nature. But validating expectations comes with a cost to organizations, making it harder for people to adapt when things do not go how they think they will.

Organizations use plans to capture and communicate expectations. When results deviate from a plan, organizations tend to assume that the plan was correct and that deviations from the plan indicate poor performance. Managers shift into corrective behavior. From a team's perspective, this corrective behavior is usually disruptive and unhelpful. Management's interventions usually create more work and oversight without solving the problem. But the results deviate because the plan was wrong.

Frequently, plans do not match reality, and maybe they never did. That is especially true when dealing with complex problems. With complex problems, more is unknown than known about the final solution. Complex problems require planning in shorter durations, developing some part of the solution, and then adapting the plan for the next iteration. Short, adaptable planning horizons are a more effective way of seeking toward goals than following a plan created long ago. Practitioners of agile development approaches will recognize this model.

In addition to unrealistic long-range plans, another problem that causes expectation misalignment in organizations is a lack of transparency. Lack of transparency is often caused by fear of the reactions that are triggered when expectations are not met. Knowing that an executive who is removed from the work will insert themselves into the work of a team when expectations and reality do not align causes teams to hide what is going on. This leads to projects that report that everything is fine until right at the end when failure can no longer be hidden.

Some call projects that lack transparency on their true status *watermelon projects* because they look green from the outside but really are red inside. Bryan, from the opening story of this chapter, has several watermelon projects.

We must open the door for conversations that are based on reality. To do that, we should rid ourselves of the notion of "bad news."

TRANSFORMING "BAD NEWS" INTO JUST "NEWS"

The solution to problems related to alignment and expectations is deeper executive engagement, but not the kind of micromanagement that usually occurs when executive expectations are not met. The solution is for executives to reform their expectations, not to expect progress to be made in lock-step with a plan created by people who, while meaning well, had little more than assumptions to go on while creating the plan.

Executives also need to make facts "friendly." In other words, they need to look at data dispassionately without looking for someone to blame when expectations are not met. Expectations are simply wishful thinking. Recognizing this is the first step toward an important shift in perspective.

Instead of asking questions that seek to assign blame, executives and other stakeholders need to ask questions that expand their understanding of what happened while seeking to learn from this new information.

Stakeholder: Any person who is invested in the outcome of a product or service.

Once facts become friendly, teams can be more transparent about what is happening. When executives and other internal stakeholders do not respond to unexpected information by seeking to blame or micromanage, everyone can have a more productive discussion about what the team and the organization should do with the new information.

In Bryan's company, like most companies, every new project that started was given the green status. Many companies assume that a project that has just begun should not be labeled as troubled, so they default to "healthy" initially. What if organizations flipped this thought? What if every project started red and had to earn the right to go to yellow? What if green were reserved for thriving projects? Imagine the massive shift in behavior this could cause.

What if Bryan decided to break from the norm and offer an alternative way of looking at a new project that emphasizes goals and how to measure success? Figure 4.1 shows an example of a template for a dashboard that Bryan could use as a start.

As the weeks and months pass, Bryan could build upon the dashboard as he learns new information, as shown in Figure 4.2. It is not necessary to start with the perfect implementation of EBM. Get enough to start, and adapt it as you learn more about the product and your customer.

The New Project

Our long-term objective is to {**A Strategic Goal**}. We know we will have achieved this when we see {**Measurement**}.

The first step we're planning to take is {**Intermediate Goal**}. We know we will have achieved this when we see {**Measurement**}.

What we're working on now to get us there {**Immediate Tactical Goal**}. We know we will have achieved this when we see {**Measurement**}.

Supporting data showing the satisfaction gap	What we'll measure to validate value	How we'll measure effectiveness	What it will tell us about getting to market

Disclaimer: this is what we know now, it can and will change frequently

Figure 4.1 Example of a dashboard template that could be the news channel for every new project

The New Community Awareness Project

Our long-term objective is to increase awareness in the community of the work we do as a non-profit organization. We know we will have achieved this when we see a 20% increase in the usage of our resources in our three main service centers.

The first step we're planning to take is a marketing initiative to rebrand our centers with clear and appealing signage. We know we will have achieved this when we see a 10% increase in foot traffic to the first center updated.

What we're working on now to get us there is a new media kit and digital assets. We know we will have new logos and branding materials reviewed and approved by our board of directors.

54% of surveyed residents were not aware of our work	Increased use of the services and facilities offered	Customer surveys and counting the number of people at each facility	Measuring decision latency and release frequency

Figure 4.2 The first iteration of Bryan's dashboard

LETTING GO OF EXPECTATIONS

False expectations exist at all levels of an organization. Unrealistic delivery dates, budget pitfalls, impossible goals, the belief that management knows best, and untested customer assumptions are a few of many false expectations we often see in organizations. Using pure hope as a game plan is not a good strategy. Here is an example.

> The controls team at SpaSet has been working on an intermediate goal to add functionality to their personal hot tub controller that will auto-balance Ph levels to keep them clean with little to no customer intervention. No other competitor on the market offers a controller that is capable of this functionality, and the company is excited to offer an evolutionary feature that it hopes will help them dominate the market.
>
> After several months of working on the auto-balancing hardware and software, there are grumblings within the team that it will take far longer than anticipated. Some believe that it is impossible to accomplish due to safety concerns. Tom, the product manager, is responsible for creating transparency about the direction of the product, including progress toward achieving the goals.
>
> In a budget meeting, Tom refers to the team's feelings and says there is cause for concern that the team may be unable to deliver the auto-balancing functionality due to current technical limitations. He tells the committee that the team anticipates that it cannot get past some safety concerns for customers, which is a showstopper.
>
> Several committee members dig at Tom, saying he is just being overly cautious and that everything will work out. Even though Tom did his due diligence in presenting the problem early, he now feels like he needs to prove the existence of problems because the committee's expectations have stayed the same.

Tom, from SpaSet, had tried to reset expectations and was denied by people far removed from the team. The budgeting committee ignored Tom's plea until months later when it became abundantly clear that the goal was impossible. A lot of time, money, effort, and morale were wasted as a result. The committee kept choosing to believe what they wanted to believe until the team had completely failed.

This belief system is ever present when applying traditional, plan-driven project management to complex work. Traditional project management is about adhering to a plan in phases rather than adapting to the information received as progress is made. Expectations are continually reset based on progress toward the plan rather than observed information from a customer. Accomplishing the plan is the ultimate definition of success in traditional project management. Customers are often ignored.

That traditional style, when applied to complex work, has been the cause of a lot of pain in organizations for many years. The facts, as presented in the progress toward a plan, are often deceiving because they ignore information related to evidence in the KVAs. When presented with facts in many of these circumstances, people often ignore them because the plan looks good.

A great degree of emotion becomes tied to plans. As those plans are executed, and warning signs show that deviations from the plan are necessary, rather than change the plan, the emotional attachment causes people to rationalize the plan out of fear, embarrassment, or punishment. EBM alone will not combat the emotional urge to explicitly follow a plan. EBM, when done well, will give you the reality you need to address emotions with objective information.

Ultimately, letting go of expectations means acknowledging and even embracing ignorance. That is a difficult thing to do, but it is liberating. Being able to see the world as it is, rather than living in denial, is the beginning of being able to move ahead and find better ways of reaching goals.

EXPECTATIONS CAN BE STUBBORNLY HELD

Some expectations are particularly difficult for organizations to let go of.[1] These include the following:

> **Maximizing output maximizes value.** This would be true if every idea had valuable to customers, but of course, that is not the case. Various studies show that even for successful organizations, only a third of ideas are

---

1. Supporting research from a project headed by Ronny Kohavi: https://exp-platform.com/

valuable; another third results in no improvement in the value customers experience; the final third actually makes things worse. With better information, teams can work less hard and deliver more value.

Maximizing efficiency maximizes value. Similar to output, if everything the organization did was valuable, then maximizing efficiency would be a worthy goal. However, only some things the organization does are valuable. Rather than producing things more efficiently, organizations are better off figuring out which things they produce are *not* valuable and ceasing their production. This way, they can save 100% of the effort of producing the non-value outputs, rather than saving a much smaller percentage doing the non-value work more efficiently.

Internal stakeholders know what customers want. This expectation is particularly hard to let go of because many of these stakeholders hold positions of high rank in the organization, and they presumably earned those positions because they have especially valuable insights. This sounds good, but there is no guarantee that senior executives or subject-matter "experts" are especially knowledgeable about what customers want. Their ideas may be good, but the only way to know is to test them with real customers. Belief in the fallacy often leads organizations to seek to maximize output or efficiency because they believe they need to produce what executives consider valuable.

"The business" is the customer. This is a variation of the previous fallacy that IT organizations and consulting firms experience. "The business" is simply a set of internal stakeholders; the real customers are external to the organization. Looking at some other internal department as the customer prevents the entire organization from seeing the needs of real customers.

Going fast is all that matters. Some organizations focus singularly on the speed of delivery, believing that delivering features or capabilities quickly will lead to success quickly. They are partially correct, but the part they ignore can be fatal: If they do not measure the value of what they are delivering, they may simply be creating waste rapidly. A surprising number of organizations focusing on delivery speed get this wrong and do not measure value. They fall prey to a different version of the "maximizing output maximizes value" fallacy.

Adding more people saves a project. Similar to the going fast expectation, many organizations still insist on adding more people to a project that is at risk (red) to preserve the plan. Time and time again, organizations learn that adding people to an at-risk project actually slows down all progress[2] and ensures that the deadline will be missed. Changing who is on the team has a cost.

Predictability is a paramount goal. People like things to be predictable so they can prepare for it. When problems are simple, the work to solve them is relatively predictable. Building a bridge is predictable, so is building a building. Solving complex problems is not predictable. The problem itself is often poorly understood, and the solution is even more so. When managers try to impose predictability on complex problem-solving, teams respond by making the work look predictable, even when they are making little progress. As a result, projects that focus on solving complex problems can look "green" until the end, when teams can no longer hide that the plan was not leading them in the right direction.

Sunk cost matters. The amount of money already sunk into the initiative to date does not matter when making decisions. Some stakeholders feel that the organization cannot change course because it has already spent so much to get this far; if the initiative is canceled, all that effort will be lost. The problem is that the effort is already lost or spent. The only thing that matters is how much it will cost the organization from this point forward and whether the investment is worth the potential benefits.

These are common expectations that we run into all the time. They are often accompanied by measurements that cause people to behave in a way that satisfies expectations. The organization's goals then become satisfying expectations, not fulfilling a customer need. By refocusing on goals, an organization can begin to overcome these false expectations.

---

2. This is sometimes referred to as Brooks's Law, after Fred Brooks. See https://en.wikipedia.org/wiki/Brooks%27s_law

REPLACING "MEETING EXPECTATIONS" WITH "SEEKING GOALS"

If creating detailed plans at the start of a project and then measuring performance against those plans is neither satisfying nor effective, what alternative do teams and organizations have to manage their work? How will they know they are on track to reach their goals without a track?

To understand this, consider the main problem with tracking to a plan: It is impossible to know if the activities the plan prescribes will achieve the desired result. To some degree, all planning is guessing. And in the case of complex work, the guesses need to be made at smaller intervals, after which everyone can look at the results achieved and whether they have advanced the team or organization toward its goal(s).

From an expectations standpoint, the biggest shift to working this way is that instead of expecting that the plan is correct and any deviations from the plan are bad, everyone expects that some of the work will result in progress toward the goal. Furthermore, they accept that some of the work will result in no progress, and some of the work may result in setbacks. They know lack of progress merely means that the organization misunderstood the situation. Perhaps they misunderstood customer needs, or they may have had incorrect beliefs that a particular solution would meet those needs.

The most important expectation in working this new way is that the organization will be learning new things all the time. As they learn new information, they will adapt their plans for their next set of actions, always seeking toward their next goal.

The other expectation that organizations working on complex problems need to embrace is that sometimes their goals are wrong. Goals, like plans, are based on assumptions that sometimes are mistaken. Adapting goals based on new information happens from time to time. The organization should expect that. These adaptations reduce the risk in the project. Organizations should embrace opportunities to de-risk, realign, and deliver value, not avoid them.

What organizations should neither expect nor accept, however, is moving goals simply because they appear too hard for the organization to achieve. Sometimes, strategic goals, especially, *are* unreachable, at least in the short and intermediate term. As long as the facts do not contradict the goal, it should stand.

Telling your stakeholders that plan-driven approaches are mostly irrelevant when coping with complex problems is likely to result, at first, in disbelief and potentially even anger, depending on their role in the organization. Many people believe detailed activity-based plans are essential to well-managed initiatives. Being told everything they have been doing is wrong often provokes strong reactions. Helping them see how refocusing plans on goal achievement will help them make better progress gives them a practical alternative that is easier to work from because it is easier to understand.

Becoming comfortable with goals that embrace the notion of change takes time. Developing that comfort level starts with creating transparency around what is happening and taking small steps.

STAKEHOLDERS AND TRANSPARENCY

Stakeholders command tremendous influence over initiatives. They often wield decision-making authority, and even when they do not, they have great influence over decisions. Because of their greater influence, their expectations can be particularly influential on the initiative's direction. And because they usually have significant relevant experience in areas related to the initiative, they tend to hold strong opinions.

However, that means they are wrong sometimes. Their knowledge may be based on experiences that no longer fully match the current situation, and they are not as close to the current situation as team members working more directly on the problem or opportunity. And although they are often the source of ideas about approaches to try, their ideas are not guaranteed to be better than those who are closer to the current problem.

Internal stakeholders are not customers. Although they can have valuable insights, their ideas need to be tested and validated just like anyone else's ideas. Herein lies the problem: it can make stakeholders uncomfortable when the team discovers information contradicting something they said. If the stakeholders are influential, teams can avoid sharing that information when they learn of it because they are afraid it will make the stakeholders look bad.

Stakeholders need to be open to new information, and many are. Sometimes, smart people do not rise to positions of influence because they cannot adapt to new situations. But the culture of some organizations, when it demands infallibility, makes it awkward for teams to present information that differs from accepted wisdom. Stakeholders need to acknowledge that, as we have said before, facts are friendly and demonstrate the ability to accept data that contradicts previously held positions.

At the same time, teams need to have the courage to present new data bias-free, without concern for how it makes people look. Transparency can be deeply satisfying and liberating, but it is scary and uncomfortable initially. Stakeholders play an important role in creating a safe space where everyone can have better-informed conversations.

Along with taking small steps to learn and being open-minded, be humble, try to show vulnerability, and check your ego at the door in the workplace. Admit when you are wrong, discuss the facts surrounding a current situation without hiding anything, and get rid of the mindset that you are holding back on thoughts and beliefs to feel safe. Do the very best you can while being open to what you are capable of and admitting the faults along the way. This is especially important for leaders because employees will follow suit.[3]

Know who your stakeholders are. Define your stakeholders, and see if you can categorize how closely you need to keep them informed. Revisit this frequently as new stakeholders emerge. The frequency with which you need to keep a stakeholder informed can change.

HOW TO DEFINE AND CATEGORIZE STAKEHOLDERS

Two challenges arise during product development that you need to solve. First, have you identified all your stakeholders? Second, do you have a communication plan for each type of stakeholder?

---

3. "What Bosses Gain by Being Vulnerable" by Emma Seppälä: https://hbr.org/2014/12/
   what-bosses-gain-by-being-vulnerable

Who are your stakeholders? This seemingly simple question can be difficult to answer. Although *stakeholder* has many definitions, for our purposes, it is someone affected by the outcome of your work. Depending on your product development efforts, you could easily have many stakeholders to consider as you set goals and work toward meeting them.

Many teams use a visual representation called a *stakeholder map* to identify stakeholders and plan how and when to collaborate with them (see Figure 4.3).

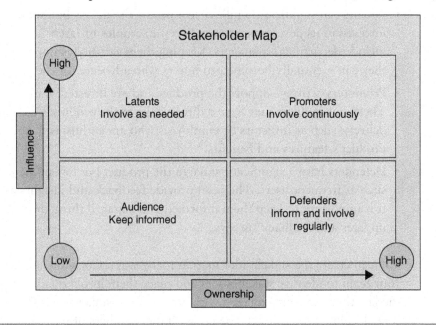

Figure 4.3 A stakeholder map identifies stakeholders and delineates the difference between them.

A stakeholder map helps trigger a conversation about who the stakeholders are and how we might choose to collaborate[4] with them. Two dimensions on the map in Figure 4.3 are "influence" and "ownership." *Influence* is the power a stakeholder has to directly impact the direction or work of the team. Ownership refers to the level of impact the work has on the stakeholder. Based on their level of influence and ownership, stakeholders can be sorted into quadrants.

4. Figure 4.3 is based on a stakeholder mapping method developed by the Liberators.
   https://medium.com/the-liberators/how-to-find-your-stakeholders-e6d96fa2e5a8

These quadrants help determine the level of involvement and communication appropriate for each stakeholder:

- **Audience** intends to use the product or service but does not have a direct impact or influence on its development or delivery. For example, end users are audience stakeholders who might be interested in the product's features and benefits but do not have decision-making power or influence over the product's development.
- **Latents** can significantly influence a product's success but are not directly involved in its development or delivery. Examples of latent stakeholders include department managers. Keeping them satisfied is important because they can eventually become promoters who advocate for the product.
- **Promoters** actively support the product and are invested in its success. These stakeholders may have a direct stake in the product's development or delivery, such as investors or employees who are enthusiastic about the product's features and benefits.
- **Defenders** have a significant stake in the product but low influence over it, such as frequent users. They can provide feedback and insights as needed. It is important to keep them informed and engaged through regular updates and feedback surveys.

You can create the stakeholder map in many ways. Consider engaging with your team to identify stakeholders and place them into a quadrant. When was the last time the team engaged with any of those stakeholders? Spend some time deciding how you will engage with the members of each quadrant. Which metrics will you show? Who will you survey to gain more information? Who will eventually grow into defenders and promoters? By approaching stakeholders strategically with a stakeholder map, you can improve your communication efforts, reduce risk by keeping your stakeholders engaged and active as appropriate, and ultimately make better product management decisions.

The stakeholder map is a snapshot in time that you need to update regularly. Stakeholders can and will shift into different quadrants over time. Some will join the product delivery efforts, and others will leave. Updating the map and adapting collaboration and communication practices will make adopting and using EBM for your product development efforts more impactful.

ESCAPING THE "ECHO CHAMBER"

Patrick, the CEO of a small company that developed software for real estate agents, was adamant that a new product in development named SalesWatch was the next big thing. He had a small team working on developing SalesWatch for more than a year. That team was led by a product manager named Tina, who was just as convinced as Patrick that this new product would be a hit.

SalesWatch had produced sales from a large customer, receiving quite a bit of positive feedback. Additionally, Patrick and Tina held monthly review sessions with internal stakeholders and a few select customers to ensure progress was transparent and they were adapting.

Internally, some people were complimentary of the effort. Still, many expressed concern to Patrick and Tina that they did not see the viability or usefulness of the product. Stakeholders from the sales team still had trouble with how to position it in the market. Customers voiced their frustration with other, more valuable, products they currently desired. Patrick's response to such suggestions was often dismissive. He was frequently heard muttering, "Well, they just do not understand it, but they will." His team, with Tina at the helm, agreed with him and confirmed his beliefs.

Despite the warning signs and data suggesting the product might fail to meet expectations, Patrick pressed on, continuing to fund it. When the product went to market, outside of its single existing customer, it was hard to position, and the sales proposition did not resonate. Ultimately, the product failed, and Patrick defunded it, excusing the mistake as something the market was not quite ready for. Money was wasted, and other market opportunities were missed.

Patrick ignored the warning signs that his pet project was headed for failure. He, along with Tina, operated in isolation, ignoring stakeholder feedback and customer problems. Despite their best efforts, they could not make the project succeed. They had become utterly convinced it was the right thing to do and were dismissive of anyone who doubted it. They were stuck in an echo chamber.

Patrick and Tina's story is one we have witnessed and have even been guilty of ourselves. We fall in love with an idea and get so blinded to feedback while executing it that we miss warning signs that it might not be viable. It is a constant struggle in product development to let go of our own subjective beliefs and look at a situation objectively.

What can make this even more difficult is when the project's sponsor and champion holds a position of significant authority in their organization. It may be difficult for you to confront someone much higher up the pay scale than you. Likewise, executives are often pressured to make these decisions and stick with them no matter what. We must become more adaptable than this example illustrates.

Avoiding an echo chamber requires an organization to create transparency. Everyone—from executives to other stakeholders to project team members—must be open to different viewpoints and supporting data to ask themselves and their customers the right questions. They must let go of personal beliefs that they are always are right about the decisions they make.

Confronting a project sponsor or creating transparency where there was none before requires courage and openness. It is not always easy to stand up for what you believe in when you move past the subjectivity of a situation. But you need to break through echo chambers in organizations so you can deliver value to your customers. Even then, as in our story about Patrick, you may be ignored. But that is no excuse to stop trying to demonstrate the courage and openness it takes to present objective data, even if it is unpopular.

You can invite discussion by using a visual dashboard that tells the story of the current context. Figure 4.4 shows a simple dashboard that can help organizations like SalesWatch.

The purpose of this dashboard is to bring transparency to all three goals and highlight feedback on the potential market, including current customer usage. With this information, Patrick and Tina can have healthy conversations about the market potential of SalesWatch, as measured by unrealized value in the market. The dashboard also shows progress toward the strategic goal, which helps the organization discuss which hypothesis may be worth trying next.

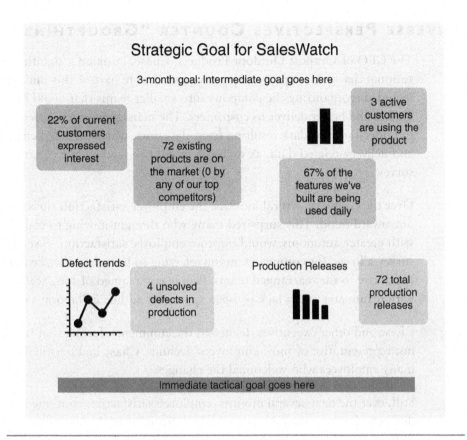

Figure 4.4 Dashboards showing goals and progress data help improve transparency.

If you find yourself in an echo chamber, get customers involved in the conversations as early as possible. If customer involvement is not possible, do your best to ask questions from a customer's perspective.

Creating transparency about those customer conversations helps to clarify and justify the decisions you are making. As in the SalesWatch dashboard, emphasize conversation-starters that will help you reduce the risk that you are heading in the wrong direction. As your understanding of customer needs improves, your attention will shift to other issues. However, with every new capability you add, you still need to make sure you are not wandering away from what your customers need.

DIVERSE PERSPECTIVES COUNTER "GROUPTHINK"

The CEO of Outpost Outdoor Products, Chase, initiated a significant organizational change to improve responsiveness. A core part of this initiative included reorganizing the company into smaller teams that could be more nimble and better deliver to customers. The management team frequently met to understand the data resulting from the effort, which included customer- and delivery-related data, as well as a monthly issued employee satisfaction survey.

Over the course of several months, the employee satisfaction survey showed a downward trend. This surprised many who thought moving to smaller teams with greater autonomy would improve employee satisfaction. A section of the survey allowed for comments, many referring to how the office layout was not conducive to the rearranged teams. People complained of long walks to meet with teammates and a lack of open spaces for ad hoc collaboration.

Chase and other executives dismissed the comments, feeling that they were not representative of most employees' feelings. Chase had personally talked to many employees who welcomed the changes.

Still, over the next several months, employee satisfaction continued to trend downward. Chase wanted to get to the bottom of it, deciding he needed different perspectives on the change team. He asked each manager to pick an employee to represent their area. Chase wanted bottom-up intelligence.

Once the new change teammates joined, a more diverse team was formed, resulting in some much-needed team perspective. The managers' employees said they had to frequently walk across and even between floors just to speak with teammates. A few minor suggestions and changes were made, and the survey results started to trend up. The team's change in perspective and diversity broke the groupthink.

Groupthink can happen when people ill-form conclusions because they want to avoid conflict or the appearance of disloyalty. Groupthink also occurs when a group lacks diversity. In the case of Outpost Outdoor Products, it could have been the authority of Chase, the lack of diverse perspectives on the team, or the combination of both. The group decided to ignore what the data was saying and instead blamed the data instead of addressing the employee satisfaction problem. The longer they ignored the problem, the more they were convinced the complaints were outliers.

Involving a diverse group of people in making decisions helps counter this problem. Diversity can mean including people from different organizational levels from different domains or different social groups. A vice president's perspective will differ from a new employee's. An engineer's perspective will differ from a salesperson's. A customer's perspective will differ from an employee's.

Chase's seemingly minor change to invite non-management people to the team resulted in true empathy for the employees' problem with the new team arrangements.

In your own meetings, look around the room and make sure you are not stuck in the groupthink trap. Do you have diverse perspectives, including customers, to evaluate and give feedback on your findings? Would changing the composition of the team improve the diversity of perspectives?

WHAT TO WATCH FOR

Much of this chapter discusses teams or people being unable to speak to their reality without fear of retribution or negative judgment. Organizations often value the opinions of executives and make people under them afraid to speak up. This can create organizational blind spots that are hard to overcome.

Left unchecked, these blind spots can result in confirmation bias so people in the organization seek to create narratives that reinforce their preconceptions rather than challenge them. Ultimately, managing and overcoming expectations requires presenting facts without fear of being labeled "negative" for presenting an opinion contradicting the accepted narrative.

MOVING FORWARD

EBM provides a vocabulary for reframing expectations based on what a team is learning. Here are some common statements you might hear and their rational, EBM-oriented responses:

Statement: It will be worth the money once it is done.

Response: We have spent {x} amount of money over the past six months and have yet to test whether we will close a satisfaction gap—the unrealized value (UV)—because we have not released (time to market [T2M]) anything.

Statement: That seems like a reasonable time frame.

Response: Looking at our past delivery data—our T2M—we forecast that it will take about twice as much time as you are suggesting.

Statement: It feels like our customers are going to like this.

Response: Although our satisfaction gap survey—UV—revealed this as a potential need, we need to more quickly (T2M) get something to customers to validate our approach.

Statement: We have the bandwidth to take on more.

Response: Adding something new will affect our ability to focus (our ability to innovate [A2I]) on our current initiative (our immediate tactical goal). That may affect where we are headed more long term (our intermediate goal).

Statement: Just add the feature; it will not cause much of a disruption.

Response: We will examine how that affects our current goals—the T2M—and our ability to innovate (A2I).

We have used these rational, fact-driven, and EBM-oriented responses in similar scenarios. However, they often resulted in an irrational, emotionally charged reply. Dealing with fact-resistant humans is common in most organizations.

How you cope with that is based on your current context and the people within it, but here are a few general tips:

- **Use common language:** Do not assume that everyone knows the EBM jargon we introduced in the first three chapters. Use language that makes sense to your audience. Slowly introduce the EBM language as a means of changing the dialogue in your organization.

- **Know your audience:** Understand who you are talking to, and take the appropriate approach. Discussing these concepts with an engineer is entirely different than speaking about them to an executive. The stakeholder mapping practice can help.

- **Have a dashboard at the ready:** It is vital that you be able to show the goals and supporting measurements—the KVAs—with accompanying Key Value Measures (KVMs) surrounding those goals. Create something visual, and have it updated and ready at all times. The dashboard can and will change as your product evolves. Keep it fresh so that people are not used to looking at it.

- **Share new information as soon as possible:** Many irrational reactions result from being surprised or blindsided. If you over-communicate, you will have minimal instances of these types of responses. Prioritize "defenders" and "promoters" when communicating new information to stakeholders.

EBM does not take the emotion out of conversations. In fact, it might inject more emotion into those conversations because humans are often resistant to facts. Be sure to approach conversations cautiously, but do not avoid them. Although we have experienced resistance, we have also encountered a great deal of curiosity and success using these types of responses, along with the tips we have mentioned.

In this chapter, we discussed how you can manage expectations with EBM and stimulate newer and deeper conversations. In the next chapter, we will discuss how to interpret that feedback and decide what to do next.

SEPARATING THE SIGNAL FROM THE NOISE

WeChill is a data-driven, streaming content platform that uses a variety of metrics and analytics to make decisions. The company places a strong emphasis on customer focus and has built a product that meets the needs of its users. Data-driven decision-making is a cornerstone of WeChill's business strategy, and the company uses extensive research and experimentation to inform its decisions.

WeChill has a strong company culture that values transparency, accountability, and innovation, and its employees are empowered to take ownership of their work. The company's personalized content recommendations and sophisticated algorithms drive engagement and retention.

Their content strategy focuses on creating high-quality original content that keeps users returning for more. With a global reach spanning over 150 countries, WeChill has quickly scaled and achieved significant growth.

Recently, WeChill has run into a rough patch as users leave in droves for one of their rival competitors. This has caused WeChill to do a deep analysis of its user base, including users who have recently left the platform. All data that has been analyzed thus far indicates that customers are happy. Even customers that have left report having a good experience with WeChill.

With a proud company culture, this sudden change from leader to lagger has WeChill spiraling internally. A lot of noise and panic among managers begins as WeChill searches for answers. But no matter how hard the company tries, it cannot understand why so many people are leaving.

As the market shifted on WeChill, the company failed to notice and then had difficulty identifying why it was losing users. The customer satisfaction gap had changed because of competitor offerings; while viewers had been happy with WeChill's offerings in the past, competitors were now offering better content than. That led to an increased satisfaction gap between what viewers experienced with WeChill compared to what viewers experienced with its competitors.

On the surface, WeChill was doing all the right things, but the market was shifting under its feet. By the time the company realized it, panic had set in, causing distraction instead of focus. It is important to constantly evaluate what signals you are analyzing and whether they still make sense or have become noise.

IDENTIFYING SIGNALS

It is not enough to identify measures and goals once and move on. You must constantly evaluate the usefulness of both your goals and what you are measuring. Your goals, what you measure, and how you measure will change and evolve as your products and customers change and evolve.

WeChill, as a content creation platform, looks at the following kinds of signals:

- **Strategy and goals:** WeChill has a clear strategy and goals to guide its decision-making. The company's goal is to become the world's leading streaming entertainment service, and it uses this goal to prioritize its decision-making.

- **User data:** WeChill collects vast amounts of user data to identify trends, preferences, and patterns in user behavior. The company uses this information to decide which shows and movies to produce or license, as well as how to market them.

- **A/B testing:** WeChill uses A/B testing extensively to optimize the user experience. It tests various versions of the user interface, content recommendations, and marketing campaigns to determine which perform the best. By comparing and contrasting the results of the tests, the company can arrive at new hypotheses.

- **Content analysis:** WeChill analyzes the performance of its existing content to determine what types of content are most popular with viewers. This helps the company decide which new content to produce or license. WeChill cannot simply ask viewers whether they like the content because that could lead to a blind spot. Viewers might like the content but not as much as something else a competitor is offering. WeChill must measure the satisfaction gap relative to alternatives to understand if it has the right content.

- **Employee feedback:** WeChill encourages employees to give feedback on the company's strategy and decision-making processes. The company believes this feedback helps it make better decisions by considering multiple perspectives.

WeChill captures and analyzes user data in different ways. Here are some examples:

- **Viewing data:** WeChill collects information on what shows and movies its users are watching and how long and frequently they watch them. This data helps WeChill identify which shows are popular.

- **Engagement data:** WeChill also collects data on how users interact with its platform, such as which shows users add to their watchlists, rate or review, and share on social media. This data can help WeChill understand how engaged users are with a particular show.

- **Demographic data:** WeChill also collects information on its users' age, gender, location, and other demographic factors. This data can help WeChill understand which shows are popular among different user base segments.

- **Search data:** WeChill tracks what users are searching for on its platform to help identify trends and understand what users are interested in.

- **Survey data:** WeChill also uses surveys to gather feedback from its users on what they like and dislike about its shows. This data can help WeChill understand why users do or don't enjoy a particular show.

If a show has high viewing and engagement data but low survey scores, WeChill may decide to renew the show but make changes to address the issues raised in the surveys. Alternatively, if a show has low viewing and engagement data, WeChill may decide to cancel it.

As you can see in our example, WeChill is deliberate in how it identifies signals and has elaborate user data to sift through. Yet, it still missed the market shift, and its competitors noticed before WeChill. Too much information can cause as many problems as not enough.

You must frequently ask yourself, "What questions do I need to answer right now?" to decide what you need to look at. That can help you to identify which signals are relevant now.

INTERPRETING EVIDENCE FROM SIGNALS

With an abundance of information, deciphering what to pay attention to can be a challenge. Here are some ways you can sift through the information and make sure you are paying attention to the appropriate things now:

- **Clear and measurable goals:** Make sure clear and measurable goals are aligned with the company's overall strategy. These goals are designed to be achievable and provide a clear direction for the company.

- **Flexibility:** Create a culture of flexibility, meaning you constantly adapt to goals and strategies to respond to changes in the market or internal factors. This approach allows an organization to quickly pivot and make changes as needed.

- **Data-informed decision-making:** Rely on data to inform your goal-setting and decision-making. Use data to identify trends, opportunities, and challenges and to track progress toward your goals. Remove the noise of measurements that are no longer relevant.

- **Focus on impact:** Prioritize goals that have the greatest impact on a company's success. This means that an organization is focused on goals that drive revenue, increase user engagement, or improve the customer experience.

- **Employee involvement:** Encourage employees to be involved in the goal-setting process and take ownership of their work. In Chapter 1, "Finding Purpose," we discussed how goals and measures influence behaviors. Involving employees fosters a sense of ownership and accountability among employees, leading to increased motivation and engagement.

By considering these bullets, you can make more informed decisions and stay focused on an overall strategy. This approach helps a company remain competitive and responsive to market changes in the market. But a challenge still exists: Data without context is not very useful.

DAMPENING THE NOISE

Noise is data that is irrelevant to your decision. Noise makes it harder for you to understand what is going on because it makes it harder for you to hear or see what is happening. And noise is everywhere: in the data you collect and in the conversations you have with your internal stakeholders, customers, and teammates.

The dashboard in Figure 5.1 contains a lot of information and data, but most of it is noise. Many of these metrics may look great on a slide but are often not helpful when making decisions about a product.

Figure 5.1 An incredibly noisy project status report.

Here are a few common areas of focus we have seen on many status reports that add to the noise rather than dampen it:

- **Utilization:** This refers to the resources (time, money, effort) used in relation to the resources available.[1] Planning for 100 percent utilization is planning to fail. With people—not resources—assigned to multiple initiatives to maximize their utilization, managers get the illusion of efficiency at the cost of effectiveness.

- **Capacity:** This defines a team's or person's availability and goes hand in hand with utilization. Just because everyone is busy does not mean your customer is happy.

- **Velocity:** This represents the team's previous capacity of a team. Velocity is not an indicator of performance or a predictor of the future. It represents the team's previous capacity the team had to do work.

- **Productivity:** This is often measured by the amount of output produced. Just because you are outputting a lot of things does not mean they fill a satisfaction gap.

- **Misguided quality metrics:** In Chapter 3, "Becoming (More) Effective," we discussed how a team can become more effective. Dashboards often include things like code coverage, feature branches, and lines of code (see Figure 5.1) that are irrelevant to a team's ability to innovate (A2I).

- **Budget:** Because we cannot print money, we are constrained in some way by a budget. Being completely budget-driven can limit the available options and create pressure to make decisions prioritizing cost over quality. Lower quality brings on the noisy long-term consequences of bugs, dissatisfied customers, and a difficult product to support and enhance.

- **Time:** We have watched a lot of organizations focus so much attention on dates that they forget why they are building what they are. The timeline becomes the condition of success.

What if there were a simpler way to approach a dashboard? A dashboard should be used to invoke conversations about signals. Figure 5.2 shows an example of an evidence-based management (EBM) dashboard illustrating relevant information rather than noise.

---

1. "Beware a Culture of Busyness" by Adam Waytz: https://hbr.org/2023/03/beware-a-culture-of-busyness

Current Value (CV)

Customer Usage Index

82%

Customer Satisfaction

3% From Previous Month

Unrealized Value (UV)

Customer Referrals

5%

Market Share

2% Year To Date

Time To Market (T2M)

Release Frequency

4 6 7 1 3
March April May June July

Service Level Expectation

5 Days

85% of the time

Ability To Innovate (A2I)

Context Switching

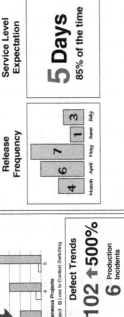

Percent Effort — 100 80 60 40 20 0

Number of Simultaneous Projects — 1 2 3 4 5

☐ Working time available per Project   ☐ Loss to Context Switching

A2I Impacts
- 2 Impediments
- 1 Unforseen Dependency

Defect Trends

102 ↑500%

6 Production Incidents

Strategic Goal

Something important that the organization would like to achieve. This goal is so big and far away, with many uncertainties along the journey, that the organization must use empiricism.

Intermediate Goal

2 months in-progress

Achievements of which will indicate that the organization is on the path to its strategic goal. The path to the Intermediate Goal is often still somewhat uncertain, but not completely unknown.

Immediate Tactical Goal

6 days in-progress

Critical near-term objectives toward which a team or group of teams can work over a short period ranging from a few weeks to a month.

Figure 5.2 A dashboard that provides more useful information.

The dashboard represented in Figure 5.2 helps us invoke important discussions to help you answer the following questions:

- What is the strategic goal we are working toward?
- What is the intermediate goal we are focusing on?
- What is the immediate tactical goal we are working to achieve?
- What are some things we can measure to know if we are on a path to these goals or if these goals are still relevant?

A more simplistic, goal-focused dashboard changes the dynamic of your conversations, helping you to dampen the noise and have new and better conversations. Dashboards can, should, and will change depending on the point in time and audience. Dashboards should never be stagnant.

BIAS CREATES NOISE

A form of cognitive dissonance is present in organizations when information emerges that differs from what is currently believed or accepted as truth. A certain discomfort happens when two opposing ideas are at play in the decision-making process. This friction is amplified when our actions do not match our thoughts and beliefs.

Many types of bias can lead to this friction between data, ideas, and actions. Following are a few types of bias that you need to be aware of as you work to create object narratives driven by data:

- **Confirmation bias** occurs when people seek information that confirms their preexisting beliefs or assumptions while ignoring information that could contradict what they want to believe is true.
- **Anchoring bias** occurs when people over-rely on the first piece of information they receive when making decisions, regardless of its relevance, accuracy, or source. This can lead to decisions based on poor information, leading to poor outcomes and decisions.
- **Availability bias** occurs when people give undue weight to information that is readily available to them rather than considering the full range of available information. This can lead to a failure to identify long-term trends and create a bias toward short-term decisions and issues.

- **Overconfidence bias** occurs when people overestimate their abilities or the accuracy of their judgments. When leads are too reliant on their gut feeling or intuition instead of data and objective information, there is a risk bias against considering alternative viewpoints and information.

- **Groupthink** occurs when group members prioritize group harmony and consensus over critical thinking and independent decision-making. Groupthink leads to organizations that avoid conflict at the expense of good decision-making.

- **Sunk cost fallacy** occurs when people continue to invest resources in a project or product, even when it is clear that the costs outweigh the benefits because they have already invested significant time, money, or effort into it. This bias is a leading cause of waste in organizations because leaders cannot cut losses and move on from failing projects.

These kinds of biases influence our ability to make objective decisions. When these forms of bias settle into an office environment, they are quite hard to break. Be cautious presenting objective data in these circumstances because it may lead to an emotional reaction you are unprepared for. Slowly combat these biases through a conversation around outcome-driven goals and ways to objectively measure them.

Leading vs. Lagging Indicators

We often encounter people in organizations who waste a lot of time trying to find "leading indicators" for their business. They believe a predictive relationship will tell them that "when we see X (the leading indicator), Y will occur at some point in the future (the lagging indicator)." Many of these leading/lagging indicators involve profit, which is what they are primarily interested in.

In simplistic cases, these leading/lagging relationships hold true. In more complex scenarios, that is only sometimes the case. An increased number of orders *can* lead to greater profits. More employees *can* lead to greater profits. A larger sales force *can* lead to more sales. More features *can* lead to greater customer satisfaction. None of these are guaranteed.

If the sales increase is due to heavy discounting, profits can suffer. More employees can produce more products, but if those products do not sell or are sold at deep discounts, losses can increase. And more poorly conceived features can confuse and frustrate customers. For every proposed leading indicator we have seen, we could provide a counter-case that proves it pointless.

Focusing on finding leading indicators is a distraction and a waste of time. Instead of trying to find predictive relationships, it is better to form better hypotheses to answer your most important questions. These questions tend to be customer-oriented: "Does this feature improve customer satisfaction?" or "Is our understanding of customer needs correct?"

These questions are often hard to answer, which is why some organizations try to look for leading indicators. Not only are leading indicators unreliable, but they are not even focused on answering the right questions.

THE CUSTOMER IS NOT ALWAYS RIGHT

Data alone rarely tells the full story; most of the time, data tells the story you want to hear based on the questions you ask and manipulated the way you want. When you start seeing data that does not quite make sense, you need to get out and see what is happening.

Some organizations hold "voice of the customer" sessions in which customers express what they need the product to do that it does not do today. With these sessions, the problem is that the needs are often expressed in terms of solutions, such as, "I need the product to do this," rather than expressions of, "Here is what I would like to achieve; can you help me?" Consider the story that follows on how these kinds of sessions can be blinding.

Agile For Robots (AFR), a leading training and consulting firm, was trying to stay ahead of its biggest competitors. Along with surveying existing customers, the firm formed a customer focus group to identify what satisfaction gaps might exist that it needed to fulfill today.

As AFR studied that data and spoke with the focus group, a theme began to emerge around engagement. Current and new customers were yearning for a way to engage with AFR and other like-minded people in their industry. There were options present but nothing like what customers were describing.

Increasing engagement of AFR and like-minded people led to a few hypotheses of things AFR could do. The focus group felt strongly that a new online forum driven by AFR was the best way of creating new conversations and increasing engagement.

AFR created a community forum with all the bells and whistles customers could desire. Over a year later, having spent a lot of time, effort, and money, AFR decided to pull the plug on the product. There were a lot of signups to the platform, but engagement was low. It became quite cumbersome to maintain and was losing revenue. The product had failed.

All the signals of success were there for the community forum AFR decided to develop. Through surveys and focus, new and existing customers this is what they wanted. Yet, when the forum was delivered, nobody used it. AFR blindly followed its customers and built a solution no one used or wanted.

AFR's lesson was expensive but valuable to the rest of us: Customer feedback can provide valuable insights, but it can also add noise to decision-making. Stakeholders may have different priorities, and their feedback only sometimes aligns with the organization's goals or values.

In addition to the blinding voice of the customer sessions, organizations selling products or services into enterprises often have their executives meet with peer executives at client companies. The executives from the product or service companies often come back from these meetings with new customer needs, sometimes adamantly insisting that new capabilities must be added in the next release because the executive promised them to customers. In executive meetings, these needs are usually filtered and interpreted through several layers of an organization, which is a problem.

The only way to understand customer needs is to interface directly with them through a variety of methods, such as observing people directly, using customer-driven prototyping, going into the field, or directly speaking with them. Even when applying any of these methods, the needs may be filtered by a customer's presumptions about how the product works. Everything is a hypothesis of value even if all signals from a customer indicate it will be valuable.

All this is critical to understanding the customer's *satisfaction gap*. What you usually get is an expression of what they think you can do to your product or service to solve their problem. Sometimes they are right, and you just need to give them what they ask for. But sometimes, when you understand what they are trying to achieve, you can figure out something far, far better.

OBJECTIFYING NARRATIVES

Narratives are stories we tell ourselves. Sometimes, they can be negative and detrimental, especially when no evidence supports that narrative. That is what happened at WeChill.

> Executives at WeChill began thinking their platform needed to be more coherent and certain features were no longer relevant. One of these features they wanted to remove was the user reviews section. Data illustrated that many users submitted negative recommendations. They felt these submissions could have been more helpful and caused users to miss out on good shows because of the negative reviews. Executives believed personalized recommendations were far more important to a person viewing decisions and could be controlled by the platform.
>
> A major investment into a recommendations engine would become the primary way for users to discover new content. The executives trusted their recommendation algorithm over the voice of the users. They believed removing user reviews would streamline the platform and make it easier for users to find relevant content.
>
> The decision had unexpected consequences. Users who had relied on user reviews to find new content were left without a valuable source of information. The content recommendations they received from the recommendation engine were not as relevant to the reviews coming from users in similar demographics.
>
> The company's reputation suffered as users took to social media to express their irritation with the platform's latest change. The decision to remove user reviews also affected user engagement, as some users began to consider switching to other streaming platforms that still had user reviews.
>
> The executives at WeChill issued a statement saying they had listened to user feedback and would reinstate the user reviews section. However, the damage had already been done. WeChill's reputation took a hit, and users had lost trust in the platform.

In the latest at WeChill, executives made data fit their beliefs. They did not listen to the data and let that information drive their decisions. Making data fit a narrative rather than driving a narrative based on data is dangerous, and WeChill paid the price for it.

When a narrative is created and data is morphed into fitting that narrative, we often find that a key value area (KVA)—and related goals centered around it—ends up being overemphasized. Figure 5.3 illustrates what may happen if each KVA becomes the singular focus while the others are ignored.

It is important to know if your organization puts too much emphasis on a particular KVA. Do you recognize some of the negative impacts in Figure 5.3 that occur when a KVA has a bias? Are your goals emphasizing one of them?

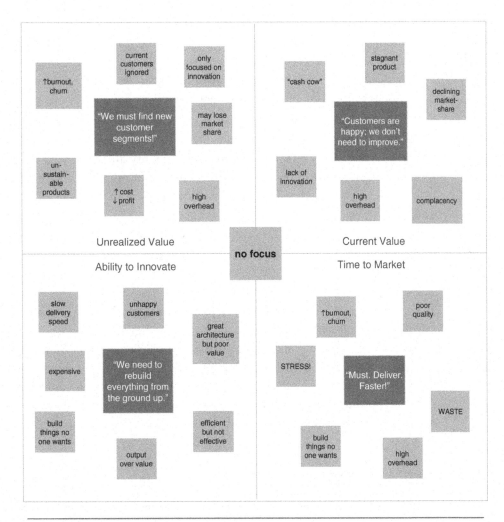

Figure 5.3 Too much focus on only one KVA can have consequences.

Here are some themes we have found when overfocusing on a KVA:

- **Unrealized Value (UV):** If you are focused entirely on UV, you might find something current or existing customers love. But overfocusing on UV can lead to current customers feeling disengaged because you are not serving their needs. It can cause you to neglect your cash cow products. Also, it can cause your teams to become less effective because internal pressures are to build new things, not to refine what is there.

- **Current Value (CV):** Current customers might be elated by the focus you put on them when you emphasize CV. However, employees may leave or feel bored because the work is not exciting. You might miss out on fulfilling satisfaction gaps to acquire new or existing customer's unmet needs. You may ultimately sacrifice your ability to adapt to the market as your solution becomes tailored to existing customers.

- **Time to Market (T2M):** Going faster helps you test hypotheses of value more quickly, making the time to validate those hypotheses shorter. But overfocusing on speed leads to issues with quality and decreased effectiveness to deliver, which ultimately limits your ability to deliver with sustainable speed. We discussed this at length in *Chapter 3*.

- **Ability to Innovate (A2I):** Making your delivery more effective enables you to deliver a more desirable result in the long term. But chasing efficiencies and effectiveness for long periods of time results in missing market opportunities in both UV and CV.

If you find yourself overfocused on a particular KVA, the first step toward curing that overfocus is to make it transparent. Highlight why other KVAs and a holistic approach may be important for your team and organization. It is okay to focus on a KVA for a short period of time, but it is not a viable long-term strategy. Ask what behaviors might be occurring in your organization and within your team because of that single focus. What should you be focused on right now?

GETTING UNSTUCK

"But this is the way we've always done it!" is a trap many organizations fall into. It is easy to be blinded by past success. It is in the very nature of human beings to avoid what has brought us punishment and seek what has gotten us rewards. However, when working on a complex problem, doing what worked in the past is no guarantee of future success.

> PedalDrop offers connected exercise machines with HD touchscreens, allowing people to exercise at home with interactive bicycles, treadmills, trampolines, and rowers. The company also provides digital home fitness program subscriptions led by trainers worldwide. PedalDrop's tagline is "Personal training, at home, at your leisure."

> PedalDrop achieved record sales during the 2020 pandemic. Masses of people wanted a PedalDrop machine, even though they were expensive. It was a way to stay fit and entertained while staying indoors while gyms remained closed. PedalDrop machines were so in demand that the company could not keep up with equipment production.

> As stay-at-home pandemic restrictions relaxed, PedalDrop watched consumer demand steadily drop for its products. Gyms were opening back up, and competition that had not existed before emerged. Also, PedalDrop was viewed to be quite pricey. They no longer had a hold on the satisfaction gap.

> In response, executives in the company were convinced that they should diversify with more connected products. They believed the answer was to manufacture new types of machines like ellipticals and strength equipment and to create different sizes of their existing equipment. They often reminded staff, "PedalDrop is proud of its legacy in modern exercise equipment."

> So the company diversified. It started to sell PedalDrop ellipticals and a smaller PedalDrop bike to simulate a mountain bike ride. Revenue continued to drop, and costs were out of control. Yet the company kept doing what had once worked. PedalDrop was stuck.

Is your company stuck right now? Similar to PedalDrop, many companies have something they are holding on to that they should let go of. Here are some ways you can start moving your organization forward and get unstuck from past ideas, techniques, and biases:

- **Define clear goals and objectives:** Organizations should have clear and specific goals and objectives they want to achieve. Goals are essential from an EBM perspective. The strategic goal, intermediate goals, and immediate tactical goals help decide which metrics and measures are most relevant and keep everyone aligned and focused on the most critical and essential pieces of data and information.

- **Choose appropriate metrics:** Organizations need to carefully select the metrics that are most relevant to their goals and the questions they need to answer to learn more. These questions and metrics will change over time.

- **Analyze data effectively:** Organizations should be able to analyze data effectively. Avoid only looking at data that fits a particular narrative. Creating a holistic dashboard of metrics helps avoid confirmation bias. Celebrating learning breaks groupthink.

- **Foster a culture of continuous improvement:** Organizations should encourage a culture of continuous improvement, constantly analyzing data, adapting goals as needed, and sharing what they have learned with stakeholders. This can ensure that they are constantly separating the signals from the noise and focusing on the metrics that are most relevant to achieving their goals.

It is easy to get stuck. Leveraging EBM and using some of these pieces of advice will help you become unstuck quickly.

MAKING DECISIONS

With all the signals and data pouring in, you need to make decisions. Often, there is no clear, correct answer at any given moment. But you have to make a decision and do so swiftly. Product development is a complex and risky process, and leaders and managers need to make decisions based on signals, not noise.

You can conduct market research to understand the satisfaction gap your customers currently experience. You can analyze usage data from your customers, have feedback forums, and look for trends in support issues. Looking outward at the market, you can assess competitive offerings, industry reports, and trends. You can consult with experts in the field. You can do usability testing with real customers to see how your products and services are used in the wild.

Be mindful that satisfaction gap data is almost always a signal. Data requesting specific features that close a gap is almost always noise.

Sometimes, you will not have all the information, and you still need to decide. Sometimes you have to rely on gut feeling.

> While influenced by data and signals, WeChill often relies on gut feelings to guide its decisions about which shows to create, keep, or cut. It still values the instincts and intuition of its team members. In some cases, this has led to surprising successes, like a television series called *Weird Stuff* that was initially rejected by multiple networks before finding a home at WeChill.
>
> Of course, not every gut feeling pays off. For every *Weird Stuff*, there is a show that fails to find an audience or connect with viewers. But even when a project does not work, WeChill is willing to take risks and try new things, knowing that the biggest successes come from unexpected places sometimes.

Everything is a hypothesis. You will not know if something brings value to customers until they receive it and you get feedback. The trick is to keep your decisions and experiments small so you can validate ideas quickly and either abandon them as soon as they do not work out or proceed to the next step because you are getting a strong signal.

WHAT TO WATCH FOR

From our observations, a large majority of interpreting evidence is knowing what questions to ask, while the remainder is getting answers to those questions. If you know what questions to ask and to whom you should ask them, you will get more useful answers. A great place to start is with stakeholders. However, many organizations rely on internal stakeholders as proxies for real customers.

The problem with relying on internal stakeholders is that they are not customers; their opinions relate to their own experiences and perceived satisfaction gaps, which may not be the same as customers. Internal stakeholder feedback can be useful, but it is not a substitute for customer feedback.

Imagine seeing revenue steadily climb over the course of a year. That is great, right? When you speak to customers, what if you discover how unsatisfied they are with your offering? Your revenue may increase because customers do not have a better choice, not because they are happy with your offering. If your competitor closes this satisfaction gap, you could be out of business. You might have a temporary hold on a customer, but it will disappear in time.

Perhaps the most critical thing to consider is how long it has been since you have collected real feedback from real customers. As that time period increases, so does your connection to your customers and your alignment to their needs. A widening satisfaction gap is a ripe opportunity for competitors to disrupt you and your business model.

MOVING FORWARD

As we have discussed in this chapter, there is so much noise happening all around us, it can be hard to decipher signals from that noise. Traditional organizations tend to measure activities and outputs without considering the value they deliver. Realigning measurement around value is a major shift that requires challenging assumptions about work, utilization, and efficiency that are widely held by many in the organization.

Measuring value delivered to close customer satisfaction gaps is eye-opening for most organizations. Once they can see where they need to go, it is easier to discuss what improvements they need to make to get there. Efficiency and speed are still important, but only to the extent that they help organizations run experiments about value faster.

In the next chapter, we continue this discussion by looking at how organizations improve their ability to deliver value through their products (and services, which are just another kind of product). Products are simply vehicles for delivering valuable outcomes to customers. Organizations improve their ability to work toward their goals by shifting their focus from features and functions to valuable outcomes that help close satisfaction gaps.

APPLYING 6 EBM AT THE PRODUCT LEVEL

Most people are familiar with the story of BlackBerry and how it was the envy of its industry. Its corporate customers—largely executives, salespeople, and other professionals who were constantly on the move—loved it. They called their devices "Crackberries" because they felt addicted to them. Corporate IT managers loved Blackberries, too, because they conformed to their security standards. Blackberries scored high on industry analyst reports checking all the boxes in rating reports.

Rumors that Apple would release a mobile phone sounded like a prank. To date, the company had resurrected its computer business, but it was not a significant factor in the corporate markets BlackBerry dominated. Apple had also done well with digital music players, but nothing at the time suggested that an Apple mobile device would be anything but a toy for Apple fans to play with. Corporate users and the makers of the BlackBerry regarded what they were hearing as a joke.

Within a few years after the Apple iPhone launched, BlackBerry devices had become passé—even unsellable. BlackBerry's most prominent feature, its keyboard, suddenly felt antiquated. And the product that had seemed a joke had become a must-have device. Concerns about security evaporated as iPhone software was continually updated to thwart security breaches, and interest in keyboards disappeared as people became more addicted to the simplicity of the iPhone's touch-sensitive interface.

Those close to the BlackBerry product were scratching their heads. What had happened?

MIND THE (SATISFACTION) GAP

Early in this book, we introduced two kinds of value measures:

Current Value (CV), or the current satisfaction experience of customers or users of a product

Unrealized Value (UV), or the difference between the value that the customer or user currently experiences and the value that they want to experience

---

Many organizations measure CV. It is primarily what satisfaction surveys tell them: how happy customers are with what they are experiencing today. CV tells a lot, but it is constrained by how the current product and the world around it work. This view is not the whole story.

People do not want to use products. What they want is what the product will do for them. They want to achieve a particular outcome. For example:

- People do not want to use a razor; they want to be hair-free on some part of their bodies.
- People do not want to buy a furnace; they want to be warm and comfortable when the weather is cold.
- People do not want to take courses or even learn skills; they want to be able to apply knowledge to achieve an outcome.

As much as the authors of this book want your reading of it to be an enjoyable experience, we recognize that what you want is to gain knowledge to help you achieve better outcomes when solving certain kinds of problems.

BlackBerry didn't stumble because its product was not good; instead, it stumbled because people realized they wanted to achieve outcomes their

BlackBerries could not provide. When they used the iPhone, they realized they had a satisfaction gap with their BlackBerries that the iPhone did not have.

To build great products that meet customer needs, organizations can leverage evidence-based management (EBM) for a holistic understanding of how to better meet those needs.

WHEN YOU FIND YOURSELF IN A HOLE, STOP DIGGING

FeatureFactory, Inc., prided itself on quickly developing and delivering new product capabilities. Product revenue was high, and the company dutifully spent a sizable percentage of revenues on new development work. Internal stakeholders developed new ideas, and the product development teams quickly turned those ideas into reality. Everyone was happy. Internal stakeholders felt the teams were responsive, and the teams felt productive.

Well, everyone was happy except FeatureFactory's customers, who were confused and frustrated with new product features they kept receiving, even though they never asked for them. Meanwhile, they continued to experience usability problems made worse by all the new product capabilities.

At that point, customers had no better alternative. Then, suddenly, a new company brought a new product onto the scene that was simpler and easier to use. Fortunately for FeatureFactory, it was a lot of work for existing customers to convert to the competitor's product. Unfortunately for FeatureFactory, the competitor's product was an easy choice for new customers.

FeatureFactory's new product sales revenues started to drop as new customers chose the more attractive alternative. The company was losing market share. It needed to act immediately before losing existing customers and its lucrative support contracts.

First, FeatureFactory talked with its customers. In the past, the company had assumed customers were happy because revenues were increasing. Yet, when the company actually talked to customers, it discovered a lot of pent-up frustration. FeatureFactory realized that it had not measured the customer's satisfaction with features.

To gather information quickly, FeatureFactory started measuring which features customers were using. As it did this, it found that most customers were not using the capabilities it had delivered in the past two years. The company also surveyed existing customers to gauge their satisfaction and found it quite low. Most customers cited product complexity; they simply could not figure out how to use most of what was in the product.

At a meeting, Frank, the VP of products, said, "We need to redesign our user interface."

A few developers pushed back, saying, "We thought we were doing a good job before, but customers were unhappy. What will prevent us from making the same mistakes if we redesign?" Others nodded in agreement. "Besides," they continued, "We cannot afford to stop and take the next year to redesign our product. That would be disruptive to customers as well as us. In the meantime, we will keep losing customers."

Frank was frustrated. "So, what should we do? We cannot just do nothing."

One of the developers had an idea, saying, "We are good at developing and releasing. We just have not been measuring the results of what we do and adapting based on the feedback. We can start doing that. And we can gradually improve the user experience based on that feedback." Others voiced their agreement.

Frank seemed to accept that, and the team moved ahead. Every feature proposal had to be accompanied by a clear hypothesis and an expected outcome supported by data or research. Regular evaluations were conducted to assess whether the expected outcomes were achieved and adjustments were needed.

The company turned off existing features that were not being used. For little-used features, FeatureFactory approached customers and learned what they were trying to achieve and modified the feature to serve that need better.

FeatureFactory discovered by investing more time in research, user feedback, and iterative development, it could identify and prioritize features that genuinely resonated with its users. By reducing the number of features released and focusing on quality, it achieved higher user satisfaction, increased engagement, and improved customer retention.

By focusing purely on delivering faster but ignoring value, many product development organizations have turned themselves into feature factories that churn out new product capabilities in the hope that at least some of these features will appeal to someone. These features—often suggested or even demanded by stakeholders—are often loosely connected to closing a satisfaction gap. The resulting products are expensive, bloated, confusing, and hard to use.

It is not that features are bad, per se, but they have become disconnected from customer needs. Part of the disconnect is caused by the mindset behind many tools and techniques used in product development. There is often a bias toward the number of features as opposed to the impact of each feature on an end user or customer.

NOT ALL IDEAS ARE VALUABLE

Microsoft and Amazon are regarded as two of the most successful business organizations in the world today, if not in the entirety of history. And yet, by their own measures, most of their new ideas fail to achieve the goals they set out to achieve. In research spanning more than a decade, Ronny Kohavi found, at Microsoft, the following approximate results:[1]

• One-third of ideas improved the company's intended measures
• One-third of ideas had no effect on the company's intended measures
• One-third of ideas made the company's intended measures worse

Or, to put it more simply, two-thirds of ideas had zero or negative business benefit. And it did not matter who conceived the ideas; executives and other highly experienced and usually highly paid individuals had no better track record in devising great ideas than relatively inexperienced and lowly paid employees. In short, everyone has a bad idea sometimes.

You might be tempted to think your organization does better than that, but if you are not measuring the impact of the work that you do, how can you be sure? Perhaps you are luckier than most, but that is unlikely. Organizations that measure the impact of their work report largely similar results: Most of their ideas fail to improve customer outcomes. The key is to identify the ideas that do not add value early and not develop them further.

---

1. See https://exp-platform.com/ for extensive research on this topic.

REPLACING FALSE CERTAINTY WITH EXPERIMENTATION

If organizations could easily determine what customers wanted, product development would be easy. Unfortunately, understanding customer needs is challenging because customers do not fully understand their needs. When customers see and use new things, they discover new ways of doing things they did not fully understand before. This creates a problem for organizations: They can spend a lot of money implementing features and other requirements in products, only to find that customers do not share the company's opinion on their value; beliefs in what is valuable are merely assumptions until customers validate them. This is where hypotheses and experiments are useful.

As we described in Chapter 2, "Using Empiricism to Progress Toward Goals," a *hypothesis* is a proposed explanation for some observation that has not yet been proven (or disproven). In the context of requirements, it is a belief that doing something will lead to something else, *such as* delivering feature X will lead to outcome Y. An experiment is a test designed to prove or reject some hypothesis.

Every feature and every requirement represents a hypothesis about value. One of the goals of an empirical approach is to make these hypotheses explicit and to consciously design experiments that explicitly test the value of the features and requirements. The entire feature or requirement does not have to be complete to determine whether it is valuable; it may be sufficient for a team to simply build enough of it to validate critical assumptions that would prove or disprove its value.

Explicitly forming hypotheses, measuring results, and inspecting and adapting goals based on those results are implicit parts of an agile approach. Making this work explicit and transparent is what EBM adds to the product delivery process. This process is visualized in Figure 6.1. If this loop looks familiar, it is because the same sort of feedback loops have been used for hundreds of years in scientific inquiry; it is what has created the modern world around us. The basic steps in this loop follow:

- Form a hypothesis to test one's understanding. Whether to test a new product idea or simply to better understand the customer's problem, teams form a hypothesis to improve what they know.

- Test that hypothesis by running an experiment. In practical terms, teams build something, deliver it to customers, and measure the results.

- Review the feedback from the experiment. Inspecting results helps teams evaluate their hypothesis.

- Adapt one's understanding based on the results of experiments. The team's hypothesis may be confirmed, but even when it is not—especially when it is not—the team learns valuable things. In scientific experiments, unexpected results are often the most powerful. Based on their learning, the team forms a new hypothesis, and the loop continues.

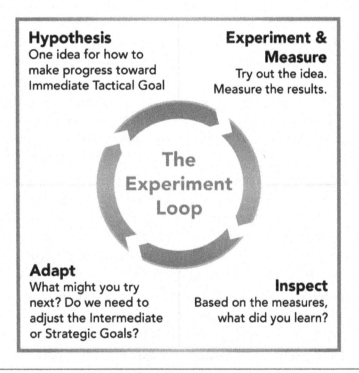

Hypothesis
One idea for how to make progress toward Immediate Tactical Goal

Experiment & Measure
Try out the idea. Measure the results.

The Experiment Loop

Adapt
What might you try next? Do we need to adjust the Intermediate or Strategic Goals?

Inspect
Based on the measures, what did you learn?

Figure 6.1 Experimentation helps teams improve the value their product delivers.

All product delivery is an experiment loop, whether organizations realize it or not. Once they free themselves from wanting certainty about what customers need, they realize that everything they think they know is an assumption about the value they need to test. This is liberating because it opens them to new opportunities for innovation.

USING STRATEGIC GOAL MAPPING TO FORM EXPERIMENTS

Previous chapters described why having strategic goals, intermediate goals, and immediate tactical goals helps organizations focus on what they need to do over different time scales. Strategic goal mapping is a technique that helps organizations connect these different levels of goals to discover experiments they can run to take the next step toward their goals (see Figure 6.2).

This example, for a ride-sharing business, shows the key elements of the technique:

- **Form strategic product goals.** Based on their understanding of customer needs and opportunities created by closing satisfaction gaps, organizations set goals that guide their work to improve the product or services they offer customers.
- **Break these into intermediate goals.** Based on these strategic product goals, organizations form intermediate goals to provide shorter-term targets. Strategic goals are long term and aspirational, so organizations need nearer-term goals to work toward to help them focus.
- **Break down intermediate goals by customer or user segment.** To further focus their work, they concentrate on what specific groups of customers need. Borrowing a concept from user-centered design, teams can use the concept of a *persona* to hone their efforts even more narrowly.[2] These needs can be examined by asking what unmet desired outcomes those groups of customers, those personas, are seeking.
- **Form immediate tactical goals to focus near-term efforts.** Teams then form an immediate tactical goal based on the desired outcome. If they achieve this goal, they will have delivered the desired outcome.
- **Devise next steps to achieve immediate tactical goals.** Experiments are the next steps that teams need to take toward their immediate tactical goal. They are experiments because the team is not sure that the thing they undertake will achieve their goal, but it is their best shot. Experiments take the form of building and delivering some new capability the team thinks will achieve the immediate tactical goal.

---

2. A persona is a fictional, yet realistic, description of a typical or target user of the product.

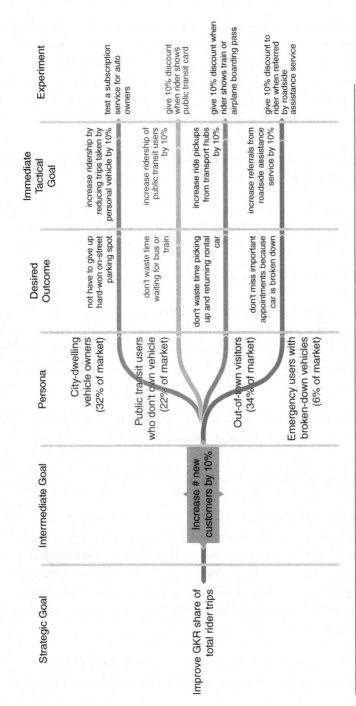

Figure 6.2 Strategic Goal Maps help organizations form improvement experiments.

Using a strategic goal map helps teams break down strategic goals into something they can build and test. These experiments help teams and their organizations progress toward strategic goals, even when they do not know exactly how they will achieve that goal. It also lets them test their understanding of the customers' needs, which sometimes leads them to change and adapt their intermediate and strategic goals.

PRODUCTS ARE VEHICLES FOR RUNNING EXPERIMENTS ABOUT VALUE

Many organizations struggle to define their products. They have complex products that do different things for different people, making it hard to say what the product really is, what value it delivers, and to whom.

Why is this bad? In a word, focus.

The more things a product does for different kinds of people, the more complex it becomes, which makes it harder for the customer to use and harder for the organization to deliver. Complex products burdened with features no one understands—but no one can kill—create organizational complexity, increase costs, and result in baffling products that frustrate customers.

In our consulting work, we have found that many organizations struggle with what a product is. Our simple definition follows:

Product: A vehicle for delivering outcomes to a group of people.

The simplest and easiest way to use products is to have them deliver a relatively small set of positive outcomes to a group of people with a common set of needs. People have different needs depending on the circumstance—each of which is served by various products that deliver different outcomes. Many product professionals talk about "the customer" as if there is such a thing as a single user with a single set of needs. This language prevents people from seeing who uses the product and why.

Complex products are not only harder to use but harder to develop and manage. They often require huge teams staffed by people with an assortment of skills. As we explored in Chapter 3, "Becoming (More) Effective," the hand-offs and communication between all these people create overhead that slows down development work and makes experimenting more complex. Breaking a complex product into two or more simpler ones by grouping related outcomes together eliminates much of this complexity and overhead (see Figure 6.3).

In this example, "Product Polyglot" does numerous things for people depending on the situation. (By way of metaphor, it speaks in different languages to different groups of people.) There also are some shared capabilities (the black dots) that benefit all users. By splitting Polyglot, each product becomes simpler to develop and use. There is a little complexity in managing the common capabilities in each, but there are ways to manage this—and using shared components is just one.

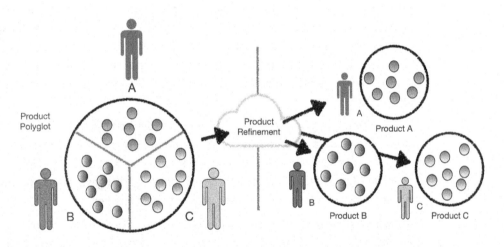

Figure 6.3 Break complex products into simpler products using outcomes.

By dividing Polyglot, each product serves its customers in the simplest possible way. Each product development team can get to know its customers and its unique needs more intimately, thus producing better results.

Of course, some products, if they delivered only a single outcome, would be less usable. For example, think of using a single smartphone clock app (rather than separate apps) that tells the current time and the time in various time zones and has an alarm clock, stopwatch, and timer.

An ideal product bundles related outcomes because people tend to think of them similarly. Likewise, that ideal product may be less costly because similar expertise is needed to produce it.

Grouping related outcomes to create more usable products that are easier to develop and deliver is one of the goals of product portfolio management. We will explore this further in Chapter 7, "Applying EBM at the Portfolio Level."

SOMETIMES TEAMS LOSE THE THREAD AND NEED A REMINDER

InsureIT was facing significant product development challenges. Five teams diligently worked on a single product, but they completing and releasing features without understanding the impact or purpose of the work. Despite their frequent deliveries and high stakeholder satisfaction, the team was unsure why they did the work. Frequent personnel changes and turnover the past few years erased any understanding of the original purpose and product goals.

Sandra, a newly appointed executive over the direct-to-consumer division, began asking about the product, its goals, and progress toward them. She quickly discovered the team's lack of clarity around purpose and goals. Determined to solve this gap in understanding, Sandra gave the team until the end of the week to provide her with a better answer.

After some digging, the team members found old documents and emails describing the current and desired future outcomes. The initial goal had been to create a self-servicing portal to significantly streamline the process of obtaining insurance quotes for customers. The product aimed to reduce the quote turnaround time from ten days to just one day.

Unfortunately, three years later, customers had not experienced an improvement in quote time. The team's focus shifted, at the behest of the internal stakeholders, away from the original customer-centric purpose of improving the quote process to making work easier for internal employees. The team had been listening to its stakeholders, but those stakeholders had their own agendas that were misaligned with the product's customer-oriented goal.

Sandra thought the goal was still worth pursuing. Getting the product back on track required two things. First, the current product sponsor needed to assert authority and regain control from the internal stakeholders who were pulling the product in divergent directions. Second, the team needed to shift its immediate tactical goals away from merely appeasing internal stakeholders and refocus on aligning them with the product's strategic goal.

With these changes implemented, the team started making rapid progress toward its objective through small experiments directly aimed at reducing quote time. By prioritizing customer-centric goals and realigning stakeholder interests, the team reestablished a clear purpose for the product. The team set itself on a path toward achieving the original strategic goal of reducing quote turnaround time.

Teams building products that have been around a long time, especially, often lose the thread on why they are doing the work they are. Internal stakeholders, especially, can have their own reasons for wanting things, such as making their lives easier or contributing to their own goals. But if the product is intended to benefit real customers, internal customers are not the best source of product feedback.

Taking back control from internal stakeholders can be a challenge. They often feel that *they* are the customer and their needs come first. The product's sponsor must take control back from them and, ultimately, find stakeholders aligned with the product's goals.

Ultimately, product teams need to measure actual customer outcomes and not rely on unreliable proxies like internal stakeholder satisfaction. Internal stakeholders are not the same as customers, and their opinions about what customers want usually turn out to be unreliable.

RUNNING EXPERIMENTS AND MEASURING RESULTS

Building new capabilities, as challenging as that is, is often the easy part. The hard part is gathering feedback that will tell you whether you achieved your goal or still have more work to do.

Chapter 5, "Separating the Signal from the Noise," talked about separating the signal from the noise. To separate customer signals from the general background noise, you have to be clear about what questions you need to have answered, and then you have to devise ways to gather data to answer those questions.

Before you can do that, you need to be able to deliver new product improvements and gather feedback in relatively short cycles. Once a month is about the slowest you can go and still get meaningful feedback.[3] If you cannot achieve feedback cycles this fast, you cannot get feedback on your ideas quickly enough to make much progress toward your goals. By the time you reach your goal, the target will have moved.

If you cannot achieve monthly or faster feedback cycles, refer to Chapter 3 and work on the techniques we mentioned there to improve your ability to innovate (A2I) and your time to market (T2M).

If you *can* achieve fast feedback cycles, you need to think about how to gather that feedback. Your options usually fall into the following categories:

- **Direct observation:** Watching how people use your product is the best way to understand what they are doing, the context in which they are doing it, and the outcomes they achieve. Although this approach provides excellent data, it is expensive and time-consuming. It is also intrusive, and people can act differently than they normally would because they know they are being observed.

- **Indirect observation:** If you cannot observe how people use your product, you can often measure things about how they use it. Knowing whether someone used your new feature is useful, even if you do not know if it helped them achieve what they hoped to achieve in using it. Indirect observation usually means building measurement into the product itself, which is relatively easy if your product runs in the cloud, and getting easier as many products are now connected, in some way, to the internet. But indirect observation may be impossible because customers will not let you gather data on them, even if you assure them you will anonymize it.

---

3. The Scrum framework, based on a large body of experience in delivering products in short intervals, sets the maximum delivery cycle time at a month. See https://scrumguides.org/.

- **Indirect subjective feedback:** If you cannot measure the direct or indirect effects of people using your product, you can ask them what they experienced through interviews and surveys. The problem with these techniques is that people have faulty memories. They will tell you what they believe happened, but it may not be exactly what happened. And you often cannot get at the level of detail you would like. People get tired of interview and survey questions, and you cannot ask them for too much information. But sometimes interviews or surveys can do things that observation—direct or indirect—cannot: it can tell you what the person interviewed hoped to achieve. It can tell you about intent, which is useful information to help you form better goals.

- **Unsolicited feedback on social media:** Social media feedback involves monitoring and analyzing online conversations, comments, and mentions related to a brand, product, or service. It provides insights into current value, customer satisfaction, and possible satisfaction gaps. But it can also be biased and, unfortunately, fabricated by competitors or people simply acting as trolls. Social media feedback can be valuable, but it can also be noise.

In the previous chapter, we introduced the content streaming service WeChill. Because the service can interact with customers in real time, WeChill runs lots of experiments all the time, including these:

- **User interface (UI) experiments:** WeChill often tests different UI designs and layouts to see which ones are more effective at getting users to watch more content. For example, WeChill may test different ways of highlighting new content or organizing content by genre.

- **Content experiments:** WeChill also tests different types of content to see which ones are more popular among users. For example, WeChill may test different types of original programming or different ways of promoting existing content.

- **Personalization experiments:** WeChill is known for its advanced personalization algorithms, and the company regularly tests different approaches to see which ones are most effective. For example, WeChill may test different ways of recommending content based on a user's viewing history or different ways of customizing the user interface based on a user's preferences.

- **Pricing experiments:** WeChill has also conducted pricing experiments to see how users respond to different subscription plans. For example, WeChill may test different pricing tiers or different payment models.

- **Marketing experiments:** Finally, WeChill conducts experiments on its marketing campaigns to see which ones are most effective at driving user engagement and retention. For example, WeChill may test different approaches to promoting a new show or encourage users to share content on social media.

To get a true test of alternatives, WeChill uses A/B testing, in which people are randomly selected to use one of two alternatives. A/B testing provides a way to directly compare customer/user preferences for specific alternatives.[4]

Although A/B testing allows teams to compare alternatives, teams cannot always use the technique, such as when users cannot be selected at random or when alternatives do not deliver the same end result. In those cases, making the improvement and measuring its effect against a performance baseline may be the best you can do, such as when improving a complex process.

The things that WeChill measures, which make sense for content streaming, apply to many, but not all, domains. If you want to reduce range anxiety for electric vehicle owners, presenting a randomly selected alternative map of charging options, each with different visualization approaches, will not improve the driver's experience if none of the stations are within the range of the driver's available battery charge. In that case, the driver's experience is more constrained by battery chemistry than user interface choices, and A/B cannot help with that.

INSPECTING RESULTS AND ADAPTING NEXT STEPS

Long Haul Trucking was renowned for its reliability and commitment to the on-time delivery of goods. However, it was not content with being the best in the industry and wanted to improve its operations continuously.

Long Haul conducted a series of experiments to enhance its processes and practices, such as implementing new route optimization software. It believed that optimizing its routes could reduce fuel consumption, improve delivery times, and enhance the overall effectiveness of its operations. To its delight, the hypothesis proved successful. The new software significantly optimized the company's routes, resulting in shorter delivery times, reduced fuel costs, and increased customer satisfaction.

---

4. Evaluating two or more different implementations to find out which one works best. https://www.scrum.org/resources/professional-scrum-developer-glossary

Encouraged by its success, Long Haul ventured into a more ambitious hypothesis the following year. The trucking company hypothesized that implementing autonomous driving technology in its trucks would improve safety and reduce incidents and accidents. However, autonomous trucks struggled during adverse weather events and caused two accidents when confronted with complex road conditions. These vehicles also required extensive and costly maintenance. These unexpected outcomes led Long Haul to avoid the autonomous driving goal.

Long Haul focused on another critical aspect: driver well-being and retention. It hypothesized that investing in driver comfort, training, and work-life balance could improve driver satisfaction and reduce turnover.

Long Haul implemented initiatives such as ergonomic truck designs, flexible schedules, and comprehensive training programs. The result was a substantial decrease in driver turnover, improved job satisfaction, and increased driver loyalty. Long Haul realized that prioritizing its drivers' needs not only benefited its workforce but had a positive impact on overall operations and customer satisfaction.

The unexpected challenges the company faced with autonomous driving technology prompted Long Haul to pivot its goal toward driver well-being. Long Haul recognized that investing in its drivers was crucial for long-term success and maintaining its reputation as a reliable trucking company. The pivot allowed the company to address a significant pain point within the industry and build a robust, dedicated team of drivers committed to excellence.

Through its journey of experimentation, Long Haul learned the importance of being adaptable, questioning assumptions, and focusing on areas that brought real value to its business. The company continued to iterate, finding new ways to improve its work.

Once you have data, you can evaluate your hypotheses about the improvements you hope you made. If you are lucky, the experiment produced positive results. If that is the case, you can move on to your next hypothesis and form new experiments.

Unfortunately, experiments do not always produce the results you are hoping for. This is not a bad thing; it means that you have learned something you did not know before. As someone once observed, the most interesting words in science are not "Eureka!" (I found it!) but "Hmmm, that is not what I thought would happen..." because the latter leads to new understanding.

A challenge that many traditional organizations face is that they consider anything that does not go according to plan a failure. In other words, they are inoculated against learning. These organizations have to overcome their false preconceptions that everything can be planned and that anything other than the planned result is a failure. To learn new things, organizations need to be open to experiments, not always producing the expected result. Innovation requires learning, and learning requires expectations to be unmet. We fundamentally believe that EBM can help overcome these false preconceptions.

Experiments can fail to produce expected results for several different reasons. Each of these should trigger different responses:

- **The hypothesis could still be correct, but the experiment was not the best one to run.** If you feel the result was inconclusive, you can try a different experiment to test your hypothesis. Just be wary of ignoring data because you "know" your hypothesis is true.
- **Your hypothesis might be wrong.** That is not a bad thing; it is better to discover a wrong hypothesis now than invest a lot of time and money building things based on false assumptions. Use what you have learned to form a better hypothesis.
- **Your goal could be wrong.** You might believe that customers have a problem that they do not, for example. Once again, it is better to understand this sooner rather than later.

Sometimes, experiments fail and goals change because of things outside your control, such as in the BlackBerry example. What customers want can and does change all the time. Perseverance is an admirable quality, except in the face of overwhelming evidence that the world is not what you thought it was. Then it is just delusional.

CUSTOMER EXPERIENCE IS NOT ALWAYS ABOUT MORE FEATURES

It is easy to focus on the product itself when considering user satisfaction, but lots of other things affect customer satisfaction gaps. Consider this example.

The leadership at Cool Company was determined to differentiate itself from its competitors by introducing many exciting new features to its flagship product. Management believed these additions would captivate customers and propel the company to new heights. However, amid this fervor for new features, a looming issue around the product upgrade experience continually came up as a serious satisfaction gap that current customers were experiencing.

Recognizing the importance of understanding this gap, Cool Company's leadership delved into the data to unravel the mystery. Management analyzed the support calls per release and discovered a startling trend. Many customers hesitated to upgrade, and when they did, they encountered a painful and error-prone process that left them frustrated and dissatisfied. Customers were opting to skip new features and stick with older product versions.

Cool Company captures the *installed version index*—the number of customers on each product version—along with the *usage index*—the percent of features bringing value to users—to assess the scope and impact of the issues (see Figure 6.4).

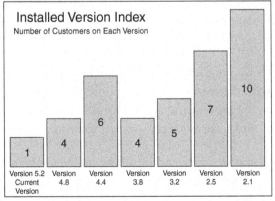
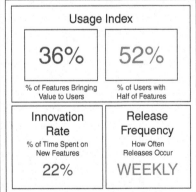

Figure 6.4 The discovered ability to innovate issues at Cool Company.

As Cool Company uncovered the pain points hindering its customers' upgrade experiences, it made another critical discovery. Because of the many versions of the product being used, the developers and support teams were constantly context-switching between clients and versions of the product, making it exceedingly difficult for them to develop and deliver new features. The low innovation rate in Figure 6.4 tells us that much time, money, and effort is being spent on support and issues, not new feature development.

Cool Company set an intermediate goal—a painless and seamless upgrade process that would be a no-brainer for their customers. The company realized that by making the upgrade experience effortless and hassle-free, it would bridge the satisfaction gap and enhance customer loyalty and satisfaction.

As Cool Company succeeded in providing a streamlined upgrade process, customer satisfaction soared to new heights. The previously hesitant customers eagerly embraced the new features, driving the company's growth and market presence. Moreover, this achievement had a profound impact on employee satisfaction. With a reduced burden of supporting multiple versions, the developers gained the capacity to focus on innovation, leading to a surge in motivation and creativity.

It is easy to become distracted by new product capabilities and lose sight of the total customer experience. To use the product, customers first have to install it. They have to learn how to use it. They have to support it, back up data, and restore data when they have an outage. They have to make their data secure. They even have to pay for it—ideally when they get value from it rather than up front—long before they start getting value.

Measuring customer satisfaction in these areas is just as important as measuring customer satisfaction with the features of the product. Sometimes it is more important. In some markets, where features are mostly the same across products, it is the supportability and security of the product that matters most.

Sometimes, improving the support experience can have huge benefits. In the previous example, the product's painful and buggy upgrade process was creating more work for teams and reducing their A2I by spreading developers and support staff efforts thin across many releases. By fixing this problem, they multiplied their ability to improve the value they could deliver to customers.

A Special Word About "Managing" Defects

No one likes defects. They frustrate customers and cause them to lose faith in the product. They drag down developers by tearing their focus away from other work. Yet some organizations still talk about "managing" defects like they are some sort of chronic but incurable disease that they simply have to accept and work around. These organizations speak about defects as if they are an unfortunate but inevitable part of product development.

This thinking is dangerous and unprofessional.

Defects are failures of a product to meet its intended goals. If product capability is important to customers, teams should make sure that capability works correctly. There is nothing to manage; if the capability was important enough to develop for the customer, it should be important to make it work correctly.

But defects do not always need to be fixed. If it turns out that the capability is not important to the customer, the capability should be removed or replaced with something that does meet customer needs.

However, some organizations let defects—really product deficiencies—pile up while they add new capabilities of dubious value. When you see a product with a lot of defects, the rest of the product is usually ill-conceived and sloppily built, so these new capabilities also tend to have a lot of new defects.

Carrying defects, another way of saying "managing defects," is simply a bad practice that needs to end. Fix it and make it work right, or get rid of the bad feature so you do not have to fix it later. But do not just keep kicking the can down the road. Ignoring defects can lead a team of developers down the path of becoming a support team without anyone realizing what happened, as shown in Figure 6.5. Developers reduce their ability to deliver new features because their focus is on addressing defects and bugs.

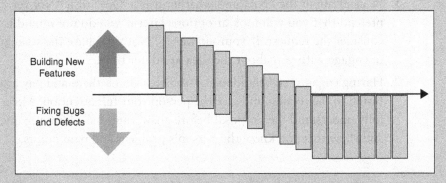

Figure 6.5 As defects and bugs increase, the ability to deliver new features decreases.

SOMETIMES YOU MUST SAY NO

Despite the constant influx of feature requests from internal and external stakeholders, the leaders at WeChill know that saying, "No" is a necessary part of their journey to success.

To maintain its unwavering focus, WeChill embraced an EBM decision-making process. It invested heavily in collecting and analyzing user data to gain valuable insights into customer preferences, viewing habits, and feedback. This allowed WeChill to identify the features that resonated with the company's target audience and aligned with its core value proposition.

WeChill also fostered a culture that prioritized the customer above all else. Their teams were encouraged to think creatively and find innovative solutions that addressed customer pain points. This customer-obsessed culture ensured that every decision made at WeChill was driven by the desire to reduce the customer satisfaction gap as much as possible.

WeChill recognized it had a finite time, budget, and number of talented developers. It carefully evaluated each feature request based on its potential impact and alignment with its corporate goals. It knew that saying "Yes" to every request would lead to diluted efforts and a compromised user experience. Therefore, the company strategically said "No" to features that did not align with its vision or had limited potential for success.

Saying "No" can be challenging, but it is crucial to do so and prioritize the work that is believed to be most valuable and impactful over trying to please everyone. Here are four strategies you can use to communicate "No":

1. Be clear about the "No" and whether it is a "No" or a "Not yet." Do not pretend that you will look at options later if you do not intend to consider the request. If your answer is "Not yet," have the stakeholder re-engage with you about the idea at a later time.

2. Having engaged stakeholders is fantastic. Thank them and pay attention. Listen to the request and give the person your full attention. Make sure to fully understand the proposal before answering. Ask clarifying questions and show that you know the person's problem and pain points.

3. Use your EBM dashboard and insights to give a compelling reason to say "No" or "Not yet." Data and insights can help remove the emotions from the conversation and keep all parties focused on being customer-centric and data-driven in your decision-making.

4. Explain the consequences of saying "Yes" to the stakeholder's feature request. Help them understand the trade-offs and impact on other commitments, deadlines, and teams' ability to focus and deliver. Your EBM dashboard should be invaluable as you explain these consequences.

Your ability to say "No" can play a vital role in a company's long-term success. Keep track of your "Yes" and "No" decisions over the next two or three months and evaluate what was gained or lost by each decision. Did your "No" decisions improve your focus on your customers? Did your "Yes" decisions put important features at risk or cause delays? Reviewing your "Yes" and "No" decisions will likely lead to opportunities to improve your product strategy.

WHAT TO WATCH FOR

It is easy for organizations to believe that merely delivering many features in short cycles will lead to their success. If every idea an organization had was valuable, this might be true, but product improvement ideas are always a mix of good and bad. The problem is that you cannot tell them apart until you try them with customers.

You may understand this perfectly. Getting your internal stakeholders to understand and embrace this is often your biggest challenge. They are often more senior, more experienced, and have significant organizational influence. (Otherwise, they would not be a stakeholder.) Internal stakeholders are not usually the sort of people who think their ideas are bad, and they often are unaccustomed to being presented with evidence that shows their idea was not as good as they thought it was. We have worked with more than one team being told to stop gathering data because it was making some executives look bad.

We wish this were not the case, but it is. The following techniques can soften the impact:

- Focus on the positive things you learned about what customers value and how you will use this information to shape your future priorities. Do not focus on the things you found that were wrong if you can help it. As long as you do not call out an idea as bad, the person who suggested the idea will often let it quietly die.

- Do not tie an idea, good or bad, back to an individual. If it was a good idea, the individual might remind everyone they came up with it, but you do not want to risk calling them out for a bad idea either.

- If the stakeholder still insists that you move forward with their idea, remember the age-old advice on resisting tyrants: Never say "No." Simply say, "Not today." The bad idea can keep getting pushed off into the future. Hopefully, everyone will eventually forget it.

MOVING FORWARD

Products are the main means by which organizations deliver value to their customers. Creating products using fast feedback loops to deliver, test, and refine or reject them based on how they improve customer experiences helps organizations innovate faster while reducing cost and waste.

Every idea that a development team delivers to customers is an experiment about value. Teams have to use different techniques to measure the results of these experiments based on the desired outcome the customer is seeking, the context of the product, the technology it uses, and the way customers interact with the product. No single measure can evaluate success in every situation.

Organizations, however, rarely have just one product. They usually have many, just as they usually have many different kinds of customers. Helping organizations make choices and trade-offs between their many products is the focus of our next chapter, "Applying EBM at the Portfolio Level."

Applying EBM at the Portfolio Level

LearnMe is an e-learning solution that provides online learning to nearly 3,000 client schools in the United States. The small company is well known for its learning management system, Click-E, which serves primary and secondary education in various subjects for students 5–18 years of age. As more competitors crowd the e-learning space, LearnMe believes it needs to grow to maintain its position in the market. For the past three years, LearnMe has been working to increase its revenue. It has expanded its salesforce and invested heavily in marketing and operations. Its tagline is "To deliver stimulating and interactive learning experiences to every student, everywhere."

At LearnMe's annual planning meeting, Greta, the VP of finance, is skeptical and frustrated. She feels like she is in a remake of *Groundhog Day*, the corporate edition, where enthusiastic business unit heads are again pitching for funding for various projects. They show amazing forecasts and goals for different initiatives that all claim to be the company's future. She wonders how the company is going to do all these things. What about the initiatives the company is still working on that were started last year with Click-E and the year before that? Will those be stopped? The company is not even making money from those yet. LearnMe's margins are high thanks to core products in Grades K–12, but the company cannot continue to spend money this way. It is not sustainable, and too many other things are going on. How can LearnMe decide what to move forward with and what to stop?"

Like most organizations, LearnMe has multiple products and many different initiatives with distinct strategic goals and unique customers. The company is uncertain about which goals to pursue first or if it can work on more than one at once. LearnMe is also unsure about how to align teams with work and how many initiatives to pursue at the same time. It decides to start all of them.

Organizations tend to be good at starting things but challenged at finishing them. What is missing is an effective way to decide what to start and when to stop working on a particular initiative.

MAXIMIZING OUTPUT DOES NOT MAXIMIZE VALUE

Organizations use portfolio management to achieve two things: (1) selecting a set of initiatives that, given the limited people and resources of the organization, will result in the greatest benefit to the organization, and (2) monitoring the execution of those initiatives so that the organization will achieve the desired benefits.

Traditional project portfolio management is the process of planning, organizing, and managing an organization's projects. Organizations use many means and methodologies to manage their project portfolio, but most share some common ideas (see Figure 7.1).

Traditional portfolio management is "what" and "how" focused, with relatively much less focus on "why." What needs to be done and how it will be done are typically the major concerns. In our experience, traditional business cases focusing on revenue and cost often skip identifying the outcomes that actually drive revenue. This causes decision-makers to severely neglect "why" factors when investing and managing their portfolio of projects.

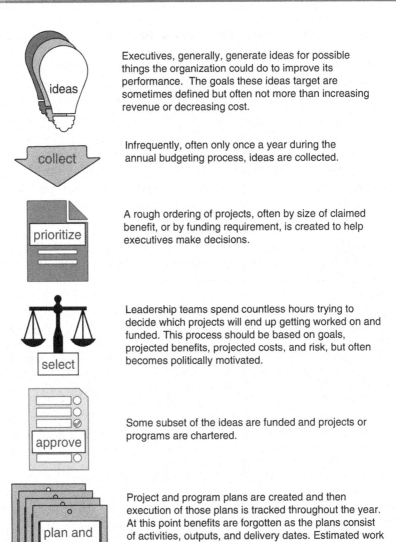

Figure 7.1 The traditional project-program portfolio management process.

Once the plan is set and work begins, people are busy and fully utilized for the rest of the year. If new opportunities arise during the year, they generally have to wait for the next planning cycle.

THE PROBLEMS START WITH MISFOCUSED GOALS

The traditional approach inhibits business agility and is not very satisfying for several reasons, not the least of which is that it is hard to tell if the approved initiatives achieve their goals. Many times, as with LearnMe, it is hard even to understand what the goals are. And for the organization, people struggle to know if they are working on the right things and contributing in a meaningful way.

Because the process usually starts with ideas about things the organization thinks it needs to build, the goals themselves are often implicit rather than explicit. The goal becomes "let us build something because it will help us..." rather than "let us achieve some goal and fill a satisfaction gap for our customers." The difference between these two mindsets is subtle but important, and lack of clear goals about why something is done is often the starting point for far greater problems.

Let us revisit LearnMe and look at some of the information it is using to drive its decision to grow beyond the primary and secondary education markets.

> LearnMe's Click-E platform consists of general curriculum learning products (Math and Literature) for Grades K through 12, reflecting the United States education levels. LearnMe considers each grade to be a product. Over the past few years, it has observed that its revenue is higher with the higher grades, especially in grades 10 and 11, as shown in its product numbers in Figure 7.2.

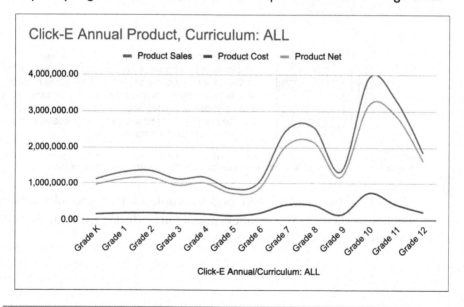

Figure 7.2 Click-E's earnings by grade level.

As the annual planning meeting continues, department heads discuss ideas for new projects and ways to grow the company. Danah, LearnMe's CEO, is enthusiastic about the points that Winston, the head of sales and marketing, makes when he discusses sales numbers.

Winston says that if LearnMe wants to grow in the e-learning space, it needs to capture more of the primary and elementary school market, especially from Grades 1 through 6. "Looking at the numbers, the primary and elementary markets are where we have space to grow. What we should do now is ramp up the sales staff. We need to focus on capturing the elementary student market. If we grow those segments to the sales numbers we have for the high schools, we would have around $14 million more in revenue annually. I think we only need to start up two more teams." He gets the green light.

But what if the market that Winston envisions does not exist?

REVENUE AND PROFIT ARE IMPORTANT, BUT THEY ARE POOR GOALS

Companies frequently use revenue increases or cost savings as goals. While increasing revenue and reducing costs are important, they are affected by many variables that make it hard to tie increases back to particular initiatives. If customers buy more of a product, was it because of the new features in the latest release, because of price discounting, or because of a fire at a competitor's factory that reduced the supply of the competition's product? Maybe the answer is all or none.

Cost reductions are poor goals for similar reasons. Many factors affect cost, so it is hard to know what causes it when it happens. Maybe costs dropped because of a new efficiency initiative, but maybe they dropped because the foreign exchange rate for the currency in which major suppliers are paid dropped.

This is why we recommend focusing goals, especially strategic goals and most intermediate goals on improving customer outcomes. They are easier to isolate and measure than revenue and cost are, providing better focal points for improvement. This does not mean that cost and revenue are unimportant because, ultimately, improving customer outcomes leads to increases in revenue, but outcomes provide better targets for teams working on improvements.

RECONNECTING INVESTMENTS WITH CUSTOMER OUTCOMES

Six months later, the LearnMe sales teams had only closed $120,000 worth of business in the primary and elementary school markets, even after a heavy push from sales and marketing.

Greta kicks off the finance meeting with this, "Danah, Winston, we have spent a lot of money on this initiative, and the numbers are not working. We are operating at a loss."

Winston starts, "I think we just need more time. Look at the data. We are not maximizing those markets. We could…"

Danah takes a closer look at last year's figures and trends from the year before that. The numbers are lower for the primary and elementary school markets, but then they pick up at Grade 7 and then again more at Grades 10 and 11. There is generally a drop at Grade 9 and again at Grade 12. Danah thinks about her own family and how her daughters were so stressed as sophomores and juniors in Grades 10 and 11 when they were preparing for college entrance exams. Her own kids went to public high school, but she knows some families whose children had to take entrance exams for private high schools.

"Winston, the past six months have told us that the schools do not have a large need for e-learning for these grades. There might be some demand, but typically at that age, those kids are running around from sport to band practice. There is a small satisfaction gap. However, the upticks we see make perfect sense to me. Around Grade 10, students are studying harder to score well on entrance exams to hopefully get into the colleges of their choice. We know parents want to get their kids into the colleges of their choice. Has anyone given that some thought? What do the customers want? I think we have some other ideas to test here."

When an organization shifts from focusing on activities and outputs or narrowly fixating on revenue and costs to paying attention to customer outcomes, it forces itself to think, plan, and work on things that are important to customers.

When LearnMe considers what its customers want, it identifies several possible gaps between its customers' current experience and their desired experience. LearnMe's potential growth opportunities emerge from closing these gaps, as listed in Table 7.1.

Table 7.1 Satisfaction Gaps Are Caused by Differences Between the Current State and Desired Outcomes of the Customer

Current State	Desired Outcome
Learning programs available only in English.	Learning program available in learner's first language.
No help provided for students seeking entrance to competitive middle schools.	Students achieve admission to their middle school of choice.
Learning programs target only math and literature programs.	Learning programs cover STEM and history.
Learning programs biased toward traditional learners.	Learning programs cater to traditional and neurodiverse learners.
Learners lack access to mentors.	Learners are able to find a mentor to help them grow their knowledge and experience.
Post-secondary learners pursuing graduate programs, law school, or medical school lack preparation help.	Post-secondary learners pursuing graduate programs, law school, or medical school are able to find preparation help.

YOU CAN'T HAVE IT ALL AT ONCE

If organizations had endless time, ample resources, and as many people as they needed to pursue every possible outcome, they would not need portfolio management. Unfortunately, none of us live in a world like that. Organizations succeed or fail based on their decisions and how those decisions cause them to spend their time and money.

LearnMe may not be able to pursue all its goals at once. It should not *want* to pursue all of them at once. It could build the most amazing system that lets potential students browse, select, and schedule learning opportunities. Still, if the learning opportunities themselves are not of interest to students, the enrollment system will be a waste.

Similarly, LearnMe could have the most amazing learning opportunities in the world, but if no one knows about them and cannot find them to schedule them, the company's hard work will be for naught. Clearly, LearnMe needs to have both. But what if, like most organizations, LearnMe cannot afford to do both? At least not all at once. What does it do?

HOW TO MEASURE OUTCOMES

Measuring outcomes can be difficult, which is why many organizations settle for measuring activity, output, revenue, and costs. To illustrate, Table 7.2 is an example of LearnMe's possible desired customer outcomes and what they could measure.

Table 7.2 Potential Measurement of Outcomes

Desired Outcome	Measure for Outcome
Learning program available in learner's first language.	% of people who are satisfied with their learning in their first language vs. learning in English.
Students achieve admission to their middle school of choice.	Satisfaction that LearnMe contributed to their middle school admissions.
Learning programs cover STEM and history.	% of people who select STEM and history programs vs. other programs and satisfaction.
Learning programs cater to traditional and neurodiverse learners.	Satisfaction of learning program catered to neurodiverse learners.
Learners are able to find a mentor to help them grow their knowledge and experience.	Satisfaction of people who had a mentor to help them through a learning program.
Post-secondary learners pursuing graduate programs, law school, or medical school are able to find preparation help.	Satisfaction of people who used the program and felt that it helped them prepare for the entrance exam.

LearnMe could use example measures to measure its outcomes. It could even measure all of the outcomes by using a survey to ask the students about their satisfaction with their experiences. Based on the results of these measurements, LearnMe can decide if further investment is worthwhile or if the delivery team can move on to the next most desirable outcome.

YOU DO NOT KNOW WHAT YOU DO NOT KNOW

The LearnMe CEO, Danah, is excited about the number of opportunities and desired customer outcomes the company could pursue but is nervous about costs and timelines. To mitigate risks, CFO Greta creates a new policy on approving budgets for funding new initiatives. Now anything requiring greater than a $25,000 investment must go through this new process. LearnMe implements this as a means to analyze prospective experiments within its portfolio.

Figure 7.3 represents the workflow that LearnMe implements to get the budget approved for new initiatives. For a new idea to be approved, it must go through market research, a technical assessment to see how much work is required, and the initiative must be sized. This information is maintained separately from LearnMe's operational budget, which funds the things it does to "keep the lights on."

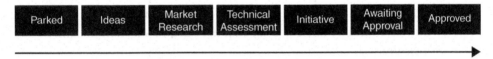

Figure 7.3 LearnMe's budget approval process.

Organizations spend a lot of time and money weighing different opportunities and trying to scientifically figure out what to do next. They also spend a lot of time determining what to measure to evaluate those opportunities.

Instead, along with the strategic goal and desired customer outcomes, organizations could narrow down their options by considering the smallest possible experiments they could run to determine if an initiative is worth pursuing. They could determine how much time to allow to learn from their experiments. Without validated information, and when everything might help the organization pursue its goals, it is a fool's errand to try to perfectly prioritize which initiative will bring more value.

The market and customers will decide which initiative is valuable by their reception of it. The data and information that an organization receives from the market and customers allow an organization to collaborate with stakeholders and make further decisions about their goals based on evidence, not hypotheses.

HOW TO CHOOSE BETWEEN BETS

For an organization, a hypothesis is a bet on value. When selecting projects to invest in, organizations often have more ideas for potential projects than they can pursue. Strategic goals help the organization decide which outcomes they might pursue as projects but do not say when those projects should be pursued.

There are implications to working on too many things at once. As discussed in Chapter 3, "Becoming (More) Effective," working on multiple things at once hurts a person's ability to focus, and the same can be said for an organization. Similar to Chapter 3's example on task switching, trying to run more initiatives than you have people is ineffective. The more initiatives an organization has in progress, the fewer things are getting done.

Organizations need a way to decide which new ideas they should work on, which they should ignore, and which low-value projects they should stop working on. Their work is complicated by dependencies between different initiatives and by unclear goals that are hard to substantiate and harder to measure.

As organizations analyze which outcomes to invest in, they can start to figure out which projects to select by considering different questions:

- What strategic goal does this relate to?
- What is the value of pursuing these outcomes? Do we need to do all of these?
- What is the size of the opportunity?
- What can we do to close the gap? Are we experts in this field, or should we partner? What other avenues exist to close the gap?
- What do we do now? What is our capacity? Are there other projects we might stop to take something else on?
- What information do we need to let us know if we should continue pursuing this outcome? What will we measure?
- If we say "Yes" to this, what are we saying "No" to?
- What do we need to learn about next?

These questions can help quickly rule out what you should ignore for now. But there still may be many ideas to sort through. Those many ideas may be clouded by all the existing work that is sitting in your portfolio. It is worth evaluating your portfolio for ways to consolidate these ideas by outcome and phase out products by outcomes that are no longer worth pursuing.

MAKE SMALL BETS

Once an organization has turned the corner to focus on outcome-based goals (i.e., "achieve this customer outcome") instead of solution-based ones (i.e., "build this thing"), it needs to figure out a way to test its hypotheses about both the outcome-based goal and possible solutions to that goal. The same experiment loop at the product level also applies at the portfolio level (see Figure 7.4).

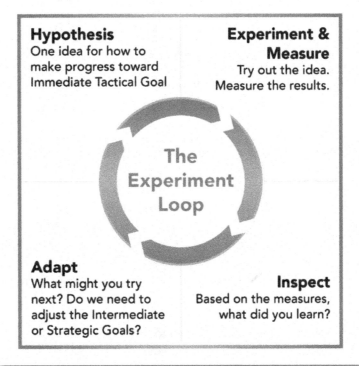

Figure 7.4 Organizations need to experiment with both goals and solutions at the portfolio level to decide where they should invest.

Although experiments at the product level tend to run in short, two- to four-week loops, experiments at the Portfolio level tend to run in quarterly loops. Portfolio experiments are funding experiments or decisions to fund one or more teams to work on delivering a particular outcome or set of outcomes.

An organization can take several approaches to progress toward the customer's desired outcome. Table 7.3 shows examples of small experiments for a few desired outcomes that LearnMe can try to explore to close the satisfaction gaps.

Table 7.3 Example Small Bets

Desired Outcome	Measure for Outcome	Small Bet
Learning program available in learner's first language	% of people who are satisfied with their learning in their first language vs. learning in English	Learners program landing page where people can request programs in different first languages
Students achieve admission to their middle school of choice	Satisfaction that LearnMe contributed to their middle school admissions	Ability for students to sign up to learn more about programs for middle school admission preparation
Learning programs cover STEM and history	% of people who select STEM and history programs vs. other programs and satisfaction	Promotion of offering STEM and history programs

Our first departure from traditional portfolio management practices has been to focus on outcome-based goals. The second departure has been equally bold: instead of funding products or projects for an annual budgeting cycle, an organization should consider funding quarterly to see if (a) the initiative's goals are still worth pursuing and (b) the solution the initiative is building to achieve those goals is still viable.

Making small (quarterly) bets reduces the amount of effort, time, and money that organizations spend on goals that are not worth pursuing or ideas for solutions to problems that will not achieve their goals. For organizations to improve the value they deliver, they need relatively fast feedback loops that allow them to try new ideas quickly and determine which ones are worth further investment.

Making your business better means producing things that help people get what they want, at the right time, for a good price, and without spending too much money. We cannot always know ahead of time what people will want or how much they will pay, so we have to try things out and see what works. This is called *experimenting,* and it is the best way to make your business successful, even when we cannot predict what will happen in the future.

The basic quarterly cycle of these portfolio-level experiments is shown in Figure 7.5.

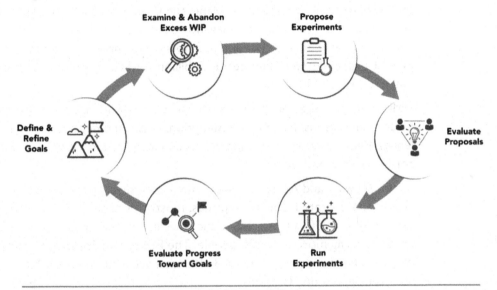

Figure 7.5 The experiment loop, adapted for portfolios.

KILL BAD IDEAS AS QUICKLY AS POSSIBLE

A big problem that most organizations make is that they overinvest in poor ideas. In doing so, they do not have money to try other ideas. Once organizations have considered and refined their goals regarding outcomes, they usually need to free up funds to work on new ideas. They typically have sources of this funding hiding in their existing budgets in the form of existing initiatives that no longer make sense to pursue.

Organizations have a hard time stopping work on things. Sometimes this is due to a *sunk cost fallacy,* also known as the Concorde fallacy, which says, "We cannot kill this project because we have spent so much money or put so much time into it." Instead of making the rational choice to maximize value at the present time, organizations think they can regain the money they have lost in areas like marketing, research, equipment, and salaries by continuing to spend more time or money. This fallacy often leads to irrational decisions.

In the 1960s, state-owned British and French companies jointly started an endeavor to create a supersonic plane, the Concorde. The Concorde was an impressive aircraft that was elegantly designed and allowed people to travel from New York to London in 3 hours. The initial estimation of the project's cost was approximately £1.5 billion with today's money, but eventually, it cost £9.43 billion.

Airlines were interested in the Concorde, but they did not purchase it for three main reasons: high fuel consumption, noise, and engineering challenges. Because of these considerations and its price tag, only 20 Concordes were produced.

British Airways and Air France were the best-known operators that purchased and operated Concorde planes, mostly for promotional purposes. Eventually, in 2000, a Concorde plane traveling from Paris to New York crashed, killing more than 100 people. The British and French governments officially ended the project in 2003 after that accident and the aviation crisis after the September 11 attacks.

Why did the British and French governments insist on continuing the project for more than 30 years and wasting resources and taxpayer money?

Regardless of the reasons, if experiments yield insights that show that an outcome is not worth pursuing, the faster the organization can stop working toward that outcome, the sooner it can refocus on ideas that may yield better results. Similarly, if experiments reveal that a possible solution will not achieve an intended goal, the sooner work stops, the better.

Sometimes existing work can be salvaged by refining the goal or the solution, but the organization is still better off before embarking on significant redirection to consider other alternatives.

In Figure 7.5, killing off bad ideas is represented as "Examine & Abandon Excess WIP" (work in progress). This can sometimes be devilishly difficult because no one likes to see their "pet project" abandoned, and at times executives stake their reputations on assumptions that later turn out to be wrong. Nevertheless, organizations do not have infinite time and money and typically cannot move ahead to test new ideas without stopping old initiatives that no longer make sense.

> Back at LearnMe, Winston, the head of sales and marketing, feels there is an opportunity missing that the desired outcome list does not mention: learning art. Learning art online is not on the desired outcome list, but when he discusses it with other colleagues and friends, they think it is interesting. Also, Winston's daughter is an avid painter who is ecstatic about the idea of being able to enhance her skills online. He is sure this will differentiate LearnMe from its competitors.
>
> Winston decides to bypass the new funding approval process that Greta put in place and funds, from his budget, an art program in painting to be offered on the platform to prove to Danah and Greta that they should be funding art. Around the halls of LearnMe, people widely refer to Winston's project in the shadows as Operation Picasso. It is widely known as a project to be hush about.
>
> Winston works with colleagues across the company to form a small "tiger team" that can launch the painting program for him.

Although some may question Winston's choices in this scenario, they are common. The result is a slower decision-making process and a bloated portfolio that is not transparent because of pet projects like Winston's that linger in the shadows.

The More Things You Work On, the Longer They Take to Finish

Sometimes, companies have too many ideas and not enough people to do them all. As mentioned in Chapter 3, if they try to do too many things at once, it is harder for the workers to do a good job. They will get confused and not do as well due to frequent task and context switching. That is why it is important to pick only the most important ideas to work on:

- **Harder to focus:** When people have to stop working on one thing and start working on another, it takes them longer to finish each project. This is because it is hard to switch your brain between tasks; it takes time to get back into the right mindset. It is better to work on one thing at a time and finish it before starting something new.

- **Difficult to pivot quickly:** If you do not find out if what you are doing is working or not, it is tough to make changes and do things better. It is like driving a car without knowing if you are going the right way. Feedback allows you to make the changes you need to do a good job.

- **Lack of transparency:** If you do not find out if what you are doing is good or bad, you might keep doing something that is not working. It is like playing a game and not knowing if you are winning or losing. You might keep doing things incorrectly and waste your time and money. Feedback gauges what you are doing and what you can improve on.

PROPOSE EXPERIMENTS

In many cases, teams on the ground are in the best position to identify strategies that can drive an organization toward its goals. Leveraging the knowledge of the teams doing the work is often referred to as leveraging "bottom-up intelligence." To enable effective evaluation of these ideas, it is helpful to frame them as experiments with predefined metrics. By doing so, the team can measure the experiment's effectiveness and determine if it aligns with the organization's goals.

Proposals for these experiments must answer the following:

- What is the goal that the experiment will help achieve?
- Who is the group(s) of people that the experiment benefits?

- How will the experiment benefit those groups?
- What is being built as a result of the experiment?
- How will success be measured?

In Chapter 6, "Applying EBM at the Product Level," we introduced a strategic goal map that helps organizations form improvement experiments. That same map can be used to frame and propose experiments at the portfolio level.

To enhance focus and minimize time and effort loss due to task-switching, teams typically suggest new work only when they have the capacity to do so. Teams do not receive work that has been assigned to them by others, nor do they pull work that is not aligned with the organization's goals. Instead, they evaluate the organization's objectives and propose work that aligns with their strengths and potential contributions toward these objectives. This approach allows teams to be more efficient and effective in their work while remaining focused on achieving the organization's goals.

EVALUATE PROPOSALS

When making investment decisions, executive leaders collaborate with teams to identify areas where the organization can direct its resources to maximize impact. In our experiences, these discussions focus on proposals that cover one to four weeks and center on the goals the teams aim to achieve, their strategy to advance the organization toward its objectives, and how they will measure the success of their proposed experiments. Although these conversations are brief due to the short investment interval, they concentrate on the rationale behind the proposed experiment and the type of evidence that will be collected to demonstrate progress toward the goal.

Suppose a team believes that it cannot make a significant contribution to the organization's top goal. In that case, the discussion may shift to whether the team should concentrate on less critical goals or propose alternative experiments that can support the organization's primary objective. By working collaboratively and focusing on measurable outcomes, teams can efficiently and effectively allocate resources to support the organization's objectives.

MAKE SURE ALL THE CARDS ARE ON THE TABLE

At LearnMe, Winston felt like he had no other choice but to run an experiment on creating an art program in the shadows because of the policies in place to get funding. He was also blinded by his intuition and his ego and wanted to prove that he knew more than the organization did and the way they gathered desired outcomes and experiments. His actions would make it hard for an organization to evaluate proposals using the experiment loop because it removes transparency that the organization needs to manage its portfolio effectively.

Many organizations have employees like Winston. And sometimes, the Winstons have good ideas, but these ideas may never see the light of day because of arduous processes put in place for experimenting with ideas. If they do, it is typically when an organization is trying to figure out what it can work on when evaluating its capacity and resources.

KEEP TEAMS INTACT, AND BRING THEM WORK

Good teams take time to form and are fragile. Breaking up and reforming teams around work changes team dynamics that take time to work through. Rather than forming teams around funding decisions, it is better to keep teams together and bring work to them.

A good analogy to recognize the effort it takes to form a good team is watching a band perform. It takes time for a band to learn how to play together, to trust each other, just like it takes time for a team to assimilate. Bringing work to a team that works together well is like listening to a band play in key and with a great melody, even when they riff on a piece of music. It is satisfying and effective in both cases because you do not have to go through the effort of learning how to work together.

Some will argue that every initiative is different and the teams working on them need different skills. Yes, sometimes, but not as often as some people think. Within a particular organization, the core skills that team members need do not vary very much. Supporting team members with more scarce, specialized skills is easier to do than changing the core composition of a team every time the work changes.

How much work should a team undertake? If you care about reducing the time a team wastes switching between tasks, a team should tackle only one outcome at a time. If you let a team focus, it can finish faster and do a better job. Pick only a few important things to work on, and do those things well.

SEPARATING BUDGETING FROM FUNDING

Most organizations budget for initiatives. This leads to the trap and cycle of creating precise plans, promises of return on investment, and evaluation gates before receiving budget and funding. This traditional approach to portfolio management is counter to the experiment loop described in this chapter. By the time the organization has done all its extensive upfront planning, it could have just tried something.

A way to break this cycle and simplify product portfolio management is to separate budgeting from funding.[1] To do this, instead of an organization budgeting for initiatives, it can budget and fund the teams. By budgeting for teams, the organization already knows the approximate costs because it is simple to arrive at a run rate per team. The organization can then decide how many teams it needs to fund its initiatives.

This change links funding decisions to outcomes and impacts, not guesses and outdated plans.

RUN EXPERIMENTS

Teams run experiments by building and releasing new capabilities in products or services that, they hope, will result in improved customer outcomes. As they plan these releases, they build in ways to measure the outcomes they hope to improve. Regardless of their expertise, internal reviews with stakeholders are insufficient because feedback from internal stakeholders is no substitute for actual customer and user feedback.

EVALUATE PROGRESS TOWARD GOALS

After each release, the team(s) pursuing the initiative has new data it can use to adapt its approach to achieving its goals. They may change the solution to

---

1. Learn more about these ideas in "Beyond Budgeting – How Managers Can Break Free from the Annual Performance Trap" by Jeremy Hope and Robin Fraser. See https://www.oreilly.com/library/view/beyond-budgeting/9781422163252/

better deliver the desired outcomes, or they may refine the goals based on things they have learned.

Rather than trying to create and balance the perfect product portfolio up front, at least once a quarter, the organization should look across all initiatives to evaluate, adapt, or cancel and reinvest in its initiatives. The feedback obtained from releasing new capabilities enables organizations to decide if they should do the following:

- **Continue to fund the initiative on its current path:** When the initiative is making progress toward its goals and the goals themselves are still worth pursuing, the organization decides to let the initiative continue working toward its goal.

- **Adapt the initiative's path:** When the initiative is not making progress toward its goals but the organization feels that the goal is still worth pursuing, it has to decide whether a different approach might make better progress toward the goal. For example, it may decide that Product A alone cannot achieve the desired outcomes, but a combination of Product A and supporting services may yield better results. Or it may find that the product itself needs to be redefined. In cases like these, the organization may adapt and modify the initiative rather than cancel it entirely.

- **Cancel the initiative so that other initiatives can be funded:** When the goals themselves are not worth pursuing, or the initiative's approach is not feasible, the organization may decide to stop pursuing the goal and pursue other goals. While disappointing for initiative sponsors and teams, this is a good outcome for the organization. The sooner the organization can decide that an opportunity is not worth pursuing, the sooner it can invest in something that may be a better opportunity.

Making these decisions helps the organization continually reorder and reevaluate its portfolio. It helps the organization make sure that it is always working on the most important goals and always working on initiatives that are likely to achieve those goals.

Imagine if LearnMe used a portfolio dashboard, as shown in Figure 7.6, that contained its strategic goal, desired outcomes it was pursuing, and data from the four key value areas (KVAs).

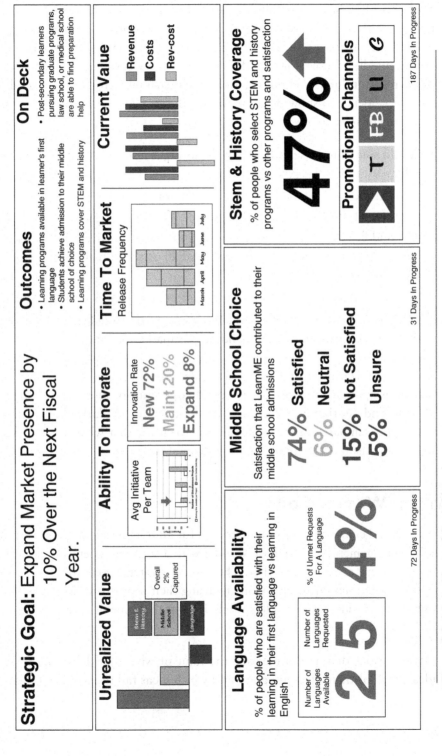

Figure 7.6 A LearnMe portfolio dashboard.

With this EBM-based portfolio dashboard, LearnMe would be able to ask better questions and have more insightful conversations around its initiatives. For instance, teams are working on three inflight initiatives: language availability, middle school choice, and STEM & history coverage. The dashboard offers relevant, high-level information about each initiative and an overall view of evidence to show progress toward the strategic goal. Some questions they can consider follow:

- Would something else, other than the in-flight initiatives, better serve us to achieve our strategic goal?
- Why are we working on STEM & history for 187 days? Is it time to move on or invest more?
- The middle school choice initiative seems to have satisfied a lot of users in a brief period of time. Have we captured all of the unrealized value (UV) it has to offer?
- Should we free up teams so that they can pursue what is next "on deck"?
- There is 20% maintenance work. What can we do to reduce that number so that we can focus more on expanding our market presence?

Unlike organizations using traditional portfolio management, organizations using this approach do not have to spend large sums of money and wait for years to find out that an idea is not worth pursuing. Similarly, they can adapt their approach based on new information to ensure that what they are working on is constantly adapting to new information.

WHAT TO WATCH FOR

No method can guarantee precise results for an organization's product portfolio management. Yet, we have worked with a surprising percentage of organizations that try to do just that. They ignore strategic goals and the desired outcomes of their customers while focusing their investment decisions on output, flow, revenue, or cost. They rarely look at the value of what they are delivering.

Organizations that do not measure the value of what they deliver have no idea which of their ideas are good and which ideas fail to meet customer needs. As a result, they live in a cycle of missed opportunities and blindly spending on different initiatives. As we saw in this chapter with LearnMe, this likely leads to arbitrary processes, which ultimately results in pet projects and an unclear portfolio of work that the organization is pursuing.

Along with that, many organizations start new work in their portfolios while they still have work to finish. Too much work in progress limits an organization's ability to deliver anything. Organizations amplify noise by demanding that everyone be as busy as they possibly can, all the time, regardless of whether that busyness is valuable. The resulting multitasking makes everything run more slowly, which merely creates noise. Without focus, everything is blurry.

MOVING FORWARD

Proper portfolio management has no one-size-fits-all solution. However, an organization can mismanage its product portfolio in many ways. Try to arrive at the minimal but sufficient means by which you implement portfolio management practices.

Remember that to avoid bloating your portfolio, which slows your ability to test new ideas while maintaining your current work, you must say "No" to idea proposals so that when you pick up something you would like to pursue, you not only have the *ability* to pursue it, but you *do* pursue it.

One way we work with organizations to assess the current state of their portfolio is by cataloging all their initiatives they are presently working on. Here are some questions we ask:

- Which of these relates to your strategic goal?
- How long have you been working on each?
- What should you stop working on?
- What may you have missed because you have been working on this too much?
- What small bets could you fund instead?

Be critical about things you have in flight and the things that are taking too long. Make sure that decisions are well understood in the company. Visualization of appropriate dashboards can help. As you can see in this chapter, you can visualize that information in many different ways. Experiment with what works for you and your organization. Be sure to frequently inspect and adapt that information because it will rapidly change.

Now that we have looked at how EBM can help you in a portfolio, in Chapter 8, "Applying EBM at the Organizational Level," we will explore how EBM can help you at an organizational level. The best way for organizations to take advantage of EBM so that they can quickly improve based on feedback from customers and the market is to consider how they are configured and what they need to change.

APPLYING EBM AT THE ORGANIZATIONAL LEVEL

Imperious Insurance's CEO, Walter, was frustrated. "This so-called organizational transformation has been going on for over a year, and we have yet to see results. We have spent millions of dollars on your consultants, on process redesign, on training…, and yet I do not see any real differences in the way we work. And this is not the first time we have tried this. Twenty years ago, it was Six Sigma, and thirty years ago, we tried business process re-engineering. Why can our people not seem to get it?"

Anne, a partner with Vanity Consulting, tried to explain. "It is the culture. People just do not want to change."

Walter sputtered, "Well, you had better figure out how to make them change, or your firm is done here! And the people in this organization better get it through their heads that if they do not change, we are all going to be looking for new jobs."

The scenario recounted here is hardly an exaggeration; it is fairly common. Executives can become disconnected from the "real" work and believe people will change because they are told to or that people can be incentivized or coerced to change. People are not automatons who can be programmed how to work in redesigned business processes. They cannot be bribed to work in new ways with financial incentives, nor can they be coerced with fear of losing their jobs. They might seek a different kind of change and "vote with their feet" to find a new employer, but if they stay, they will fight change they do not believe in.

Organizations can have all the offsite strategy meetings and team-building workshops they want, but none of these foster change in an organization. Neither do lavish kick-off meetings nor motivational wall posters. These approaches sometimes create a superficial facade of change, especially when employees think it is socially required to express enthusiasm for the change. Still, they do not work in a fundamentally different way.

WHY CHANGE EFFORTS FAIL

We have seen numerous organizational change initiatives. Most of them fail to instill lasting change. They consume a lot of time and money. They change the organization a little, but most organizations revert to more or less the state in which they started. They do so, from our perspective, for a variety of reasons:

- **They lack a compelling "why."** They are only vaguely connected to the organization's mission. Many are focused on adopting some sort of process, such as Six Sigma or Agile. Adopting a process is a means to an end, and when the initiative is unconnected to the organization's mission, people are unmotivated to change. Improving profitability, increasing revenue, and becoming more competitive are important goals. Still, unless they are connected in an existential way to the mission of the organization, goals like these do not motivate fundamental change.

  It is worth noting many organizations lack a mission. Yes, they have something they call a mission, but it is little more than an empty tagline. There is no compelling reason for its existence. But that is a different topic and not one for this book.

- **Leaders signal that the change is not that important.** People in the organization take their cues from executives. Change often means sacrifice and compromise. When executives signal that they are not changing and it is up to everyone else to change, they signal that the change is unimportant.

When change is painful, leaders need to signal that they are willing to sacrifice along with everyone else.

- **Leaders say one thing and reward something else.** Organizations are not so much "machines for getting things done" as they are a social reward system that happens to get work done as a by-product. Employees are rewarded in several ways: through salary and bonuses, but also through recognition and status. People take their cues from these reward signals and adapt their behavior accordingly.

- **Change is treated like a one-time event.** Change is an ongoing effort that always continues. Failing to sustain the change and allowing an organization to revert to old ways of doing things can undermine the long-term success of the initiative. Change and the desire to change persist in any organization that is always focused on its mission.

- **Employees are cynical about change.** They have seen change initiatives come and go, just like they have seen the leaders who initiate those initiatives come and go. They know from experience that if they simply wait, the current initiative will fail, just like all the ones that came before it.

- **They quit when the going gets tough.** Change, new processes, or different ways of working seem great until organizations face tough circumstances such as difficult financial times, a pandemic, or a staple executive departing. Instead of sticking with those changes, organizations will revert right back to old ways of thinking because they worked in the past.

We are cynical about most traditional approaches to changing organizations. They seek to change people from the outside, to make them do something they do not want to do. We are not saying this approach cannot work, only that in our combined experience, we have never seen it work. Nevertheless, in this chapter, we explore the important points an organization needs to consider if it wants to truly morph into a version of itself that it is more likely to sustain in the future.

To Initiate Change, Give People a "Why"

Remember Cindy from Medical Device Corporation back in Chapter 1, "Finding Purpose"? She revised her organization's strategic goal in such a way that it inspired and motivated everyone on a mission to help patients live better lives. She framed the "why?" around getting a grandmother back to her family as soon as possible by creating better surgical outcomes with their medical device products and procedures.

Cindy did not run a workshop, conduct an offsite meeting, or organize trust-fall sessions. She told a compelling story about how the world could be better because of the work the company was doing. She created a compelling mission (get Grandma home) and expressed that mission with a story that resonated with everyone in the room.

This heartfelt story had a much bigger impact than her initial attempt at sharing the corporate goals with the company.

> We need to regain the competitive edge from our competitors. We must show we can release new innovations faster than any other company. To that end, we need to patent and release a new knee replacement technology next year. In the interest of showing positive returns to our shareholders, this product also needs to be net positive by the second half of the year.

Helping Grandma get back to her family also achieves the goals outlined, which is why it is so important to keep the customer and satisfaction gaps in mind. The difference is that Grandma is far more important to people than an abstract goal like increasing shareholder value.

ASSESS WHERE THE ORGANIZATION IS TODAY

Without introduction or warning, John, the VP of development, asked, "Why is delivery hard?" The question hung in the air briefly as the entire development staff waited for someone to speak first. Finally, a developer said, "We do not have the right tools and have to do way too many things manually." Another developer suggested, "We are assigned to too many projects. We cannot focus and never get to finish anything." John was smiling. "Great, what else?" he asked. For the next two hours, the developers shared everything they felt slowed down development.

The meeting was tiring, but it revealed some insights John needed to understand how his division was doing. Over the previous few weeks, John had gathered release frequency (Time to Market), employee satisfaction

(Current Value), customer feature usage (Current Value), and context switching (Ability to Innovate) metrics, but he wanted to see if the narrative from the developers could validate what the data was showing.

With the combined narrative and data, John can confidently work within his organization to improve how they work with indicators that the changes are having the desired impact.

With the story and the data together, John could baseline how well his organization was working today and where the bottlenecks and impediments were for his teams. He hypothesized that by fixing the impediments uncovered by his teams, effectiveness, and delivery would improve. By establishing a baseline, this was possible to prove.

To Benchmark or Not?

Some organizations seeking to improve their performance seek to learn from other more successful organizations. They love case studies. They will visit the "high performer" to understand what special practices make them high performers and then return to their own company and try to apply those same practices. These efforts are, at best, a distraction. At worst, they are a complete waste of time.

The reasons for this are complex and varied, but they follow a pattern: There are no shortcuts to improving an organization's performance. Organizations need to form a compelling, customer-focused mission. They must form short-, medium-, and long-term goals that help them work toward their mission. Because the path to achieving their goals is long and uncertain, organizations have to experiment to make progress. High performers tend to have motivated, engaged, and empowered team members.

Benchmarking's fundamental flaw is an assumption that there are "best practices" that lead to predictable positive results. There are not. Different things work for different teams and organizations, depending on where they are now and where they need to go. "Best practices" and "universal dashboards" do not exist. You cannot copy your way to success. You must find your own way. Hopefully, that is a path you want to take.

Some people reject this idea. They say that there is no reason to "reinvent the wheel." The wheel metaphor is inept, however. The right metaphor is a journey, but one in which everyone has a different starting point, a different endpoint, and a different path between the two.

It also sometimes turns out that the self-proclaimed and high-performing company is not as good as it claims to be. No one is perfect, and everyone has challenges. Even the best performing teams and organizations we have worked with have had constant struggles with one problem or another. Their journeys have never ended, and their high performance was usually just a point in time. Even high-performing organizations are just one bad C-level hire, one misguided company strategy decision, or one more-astute competitor away from mediocrity.

We do not say this to discourage you from trying. We just want you to be realistic. Your journey will never end, and it will not get easier. But you do get better at it, and some things do become easier, but that lets you tackle tougher challenges. The best way to improve is to benchmark against yourself. Compare where you are today to where you want to be. Set goals based on the gap between where you are and where you want to be. Then work toward those goals.

EMPOWERMENT TAKES TRUST, TRANSPARENCY, AND TIME

Back at Imperious Insurance, Walter was on a tear again. "Why can we not make decisions faster? We have told our teams that they are empowered to make decisions, yet no one seems to take any initiative!"

Evie, the partner with Evidential Enterprises, the firm brought in to replace Vanity Consulting, pushed back, "You chastised and berated the last team that tried to make product decisions without clearance from the VPs of product management and product marketing. The team felt it had a good experiment to test what customers needed, and you let your department heads put those experiments to an end until they could review them and decide whether the team should proceed. The team is still waiting."

It is easy to think of empowering people as granting a wish: you just tell them that they are empowered, and that is it. But empowerment is like a complex dance between two parties. The party with power has to willingly let go of a little bit of power, transferring it to another party. In doing so, the empowering party needs to trust that the empowered party is going to make good decisions. The empowering party cannot step in just because they do not like what is going on. The empowered party will not always make good decisions, but if it is transparent about its decisions, the empowering party can help the empowered party improve.

Empowerment is not one-sided; the party receiving power has to willingly accept it. It needs to trust that it is able to decide as it sees best and trust that it is not being set up to fail. It has to be willing to make some mistakes but be transparent about them so that it can learn and improve.

The trust relationship between the two parties also has to complete a loop. The person granting power has to experience their trust being rewarded by transparency into the decisions that teams are making (see Figure 8.1). The decisions themselves need to be sound and reasonable, even when they do not always produce the hoped-for result. In an uncertain world, things do not always work out the way people hope, but if people are transparent about their decisions, the process by which they reached them, the data they used, and the results they achieved, they can learn from their experiences.

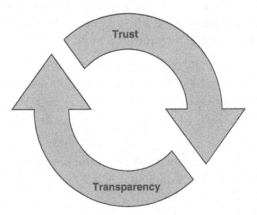

Figure 8.1 Transparency requires trust, but trust also requires transparency.

BENEFITS OF EMPOWERING TEAMS

Letting go of decision-making authority is tough. It challenges the essence of what most managers see as their job and likely their identity. Without a compelling alternative, managers tend to hold onto power. When they give up power, they regain a different kind of power: greater influence and, over time, better results. Shifting at least some decision-making responsibilities to teams has additional benefits:

- **Managers are free to improve the organization to help it better support teams.** Consider the earlier story about VP John asking his developers what made delivery difficult. What if John could focus his time and energy on removing the blockers and issues that slowed the team down? Not only would delivery speed and frequency improve, but the team would likely be happier and more productive.

- **Flatter organizational structures help teams be more responsive to change.** When they have decision-making authority, teams can make timely decisions without waiting for approvals from the many layers of management. Organizations can be opportunistic in the market, innovate, and stay ahead of the competition.

- **Flatter organizational structures help teams feel a greater sense of ownership over work.** People are motivated to contribute their best efforts. This increased engagement leads to higher job satisfaction, reduced turnover, and a more engaged workforce.

- **Employees have direct access to information and can collaborate more effectively toward shared goals.** This facilitates cross-functional collaboration, enabling diverse perspectives and expertise for innovation and problem-solving. Ideas and solutions can be implemented more rapidly, fostering a culture of delivery and continuous improvement.

- **Flatter structures shorten decision-making paths.** With fewer layers of management, decisions come more quickly, which reduces bottlenecks and improves delivery. This agility allows organizations to adapt to market dynamics and customer needs more effectively.

MEASURING EMPOWERMENT

We can say that teams and people are empowered, but there is an easy test to see if they really are. Can a team make decisions on its own without having to run the decision "up the chain"? If a team has to get someone else's approval, it is not empowered.

Many of the benefits of moving to empowered teams and a flatter organizational structure are rooted in reducing *decision latency* or the time it takes for an organization to respond to a new business opportunity. By reducing decision latency, organizations can move faster and gain significant flexibility and options in how they respond when opportunities occur.[1]

Decision latency is an important way organizations can measure the degree to which their teams are empowered. If decisions take a long time to make and must bubble up through layers of the organization, teams are not very empowered.

GROWING EMPOWERMENT

Empowering teams does not mean that teams are suddenly free to make any decision they wish. Some decisions, such as large financial or legal commitments, are almost always the domain of executives. But smaller decisions, such as how the team works, when team members take vacations, and even what the team builds, show growing degrees of team empowerment to make decisions.

Managers who want to grow team empowerment help teams start small and grow their decision-making skills over time. In exchange for complete transparency, managers need to create a safe space in which teams can make decisions and not be punished for ones that are ill-considered or do not work out the way the team had hoped. For a team to improve, it needs the space to make mistakes but then learn from them.

To do this, both teams and managers must embrace transparency, *especially* when it makes people uncomfortable.

Transparency about a team's Ability to Innovate (A2I) may reveal that the organization's structure is not very effective, such as when a team experiences a high degree of interruptions to handle other work. Or it may reveal that a

---

1. Jim Johnson from Standish Group explains decision latency theory in this video: www.agileuprising. com/2021/03/14/decision-latency-theory-with-jim-johnson/

team has made poor technical choices that it needs to cope with to better enable delivery.

Transparency about Time to Market (T2M) may reveal a slow, cumbersome, and bureaucratic product release process that is not justified by the benefits it achieves. Likewise, it could show that the team has not taken advantage of tooling that enables it to release valuable product increments more frequently.

Transparency about Current Value (CV) may reveal that a big new product feature lobbied for by an important executive fell flat with customers. Then, it may show that the immediate tactical goals chosen by the team did not result in the intended customer outcome.

Transparency about Unrealized Value (UV) may reveal that the company's long-held mission no longer resonates with its customers. As teams pursue their intermediate goals, the feedback they obtain may help them realize the customer's needs have changed, and that the organization's direction needs to adapt.

None of these things should result in judgment or criticism. The moment they do, transparency will cease, and everyone in the organization will spend great amounts of time and effort making things look fine when they are not. Transparency is a powerful tool for improvement but only when used non-judgmentally. Transparency reveals opportunities for improvement. People should be recognized and rewarded for revealing where things could have gone better. It is the only way anyone will improve.

INVERTING THE ORGANIZATION TO SUPPORT EMPOWERMENT

The trust-transparency loop shown in Figure 8.1 implies that as teams take on more responsibility for decisions, managers shift their responsibilities from making those decisions to helping teams grow their ability to make decisions. This leads to a shift in the way the organization works. It starts as a primarily top-down organization shown at the left in Figure 8.2, with executives at the top and, implicitly, customers at the bottom. It shifts to the organizational structure shown on the right, with customers and the employees with whom they interact at the top, and managers and executives at the bottom but supporting the rest of the organization. We think of the organization on the left, the traditional organization, as being management-driven. In contrast, the organization on the right is customer-driven.

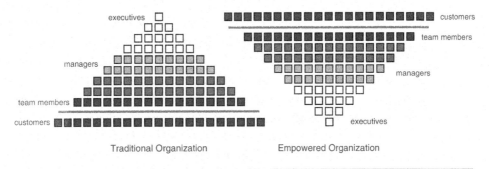

Figure 8.2 Comparing management-driven and customer-driven organizations.

We often encounter questions from managers who ask, "What do I do if the team can make its own decisions?" The answer is simple but points to a profound change in the work of managers: Managers of empowered teams focus on helping the organization improve. Freed from having to make decisions, they focus on optimizing the organization to seek toward its mission.

Framed this way, we ask managers if they think is a simple job, and their answer is always, "No, that is a *huge* and complex job that never really ends." And so, they have their answer.

REDUCING CONTEXT SWITCHING

Traditional organizations struggle to form cohesive, dedicated, self-sufficient teams. When they assign people to multiple teams, they fragment the teams and make it harder for them to get work done. Having people working on many teams may seem efficient, but it slows everything down. We have encountered more than one organization where team members worked on three, four, or five teams. It took a meeting to schedule a meeting, usually weeks away.

Daria, a developer on Team Tortoise, came into the team room exasperated. "I cannot seem to get anything done. Every day this week, I have had one interruption after another. First, it is a product manager wanting me to take a look at her idea for a new product. Then, it is some emergency bug fix on a product I worked on two years ago that does not even have a team anymore. Then, it is a meeting with information security complaining that we have not filed our risk analysis report. Every time I get my head back to where it needs to be to develop the new feature we are working on, I get interrupted."

Ana shakes her head, "Same with me. Management seems to think we can handle all this extra work in our "spare time." I try to explain that there is no "spare time." And they wonder why this work takes so long..."

Every time team members switch from one project to another or one team's meeting to another, they switch context. Team members are less effective while they are switching contexts. If they go from meeting to meeting, they can lose up to a third of an hour of the new meeting because they are still thinking about the previous one. And that assumes a level of focus. Sometimes, when people are working on multiple projects and they hit a level of resistance in one, they switch to work on something else, potentially avoiding issues. Cumulatively, organizations who do this are "leaking" brain power and risking burning out employees. It is neither efficient nor effective.

The answer to this problem is to dedicate people to one team. They will be more effective and more productive because they do not spend time switching contexts. We have heard managers argue that they cannot do this because they need to work on multiple projects simultaneously and are fooling themselves about the amount of valuable work they get done because they forget about context-switching. If they dedicated people to a single team that first worked on one project to completion, then another, and then another, the team would get all the projects done *sooner* than they would have if they had been context switching. And some of the projects would get done *dramatically sooner.*

GROWING SELF-SUFFICIENT TEAMS

Teams are also burdened by a related problem: waiting for people outside the team to be available, usually because they lack the skills within the team. This waiting increases the team's T2M. They can fill this time with other work, but this effort is often wasted because they lack the expertise to make the right choices.

> Legacy Telecom (LTC) has long existed in the heavily regulated telecommunications market. The company identified some satisfaction gaps to pursue and wanted to branch out into the exciting and emerging market of team collaboration tools and services. LTC had always struggled with long delivery cycles, which it hypothesized would limit its ability to enter the new, exciting market opportunity. It created improvement experiments to automate its build, test, and deployment processes with the idea that it could deliver more quickly.
>
> At the suggestion of Bob, one of the team members, the team analyzed where it was spending its time. Bob and the team did so by breaking out the time each task took, the time they spent waiting on someone outside the team to be available, and the time it took for someone outside the team to make a decision for the team.
>
> The analysis by Bob and the team produced a surprising result: Most of their delivery cycle was spent waiting for someone else to make a decision (almost 70%). Learning that they spent less than 6% of their time building and testing the product was especially remarkable.
>
> Waiting for decisions was a relic of LTC's history as a telecommunications company. LTC was structured where one group owned the data centers, another group owned the network, and another group managed procurement. Getting something as simple as a new computer for a developer took weeks. Approving a new version of a product for release took weeks at best but often took months.
>
> Jenny, one of Bob's teammates, expressed frustration: "Our competitors do not have to wait like this; some of them release many times a day. How are we ever going to release these new, competitive products when even simple decisions take weeks?" How LTC was ever going to make this possible was a looming, unanswered question at the time.

In this example, the team's lack of empowerment to make certain decisions impeded its ability to get things done. The team spent most of its time waiting for someone else to make a decision. The organization's structure was working against the team as the approval chain spanned across multiple departments.

> LTC ended up empowering its teams by removing the boundaries between them so they could combine all the skills they needed from data centers, network, and procurement, regardless of the hierarchical structure that had been in place for many years. This increased their decision-making authority and autonomy, which improved their speed and effectiveness at delivering valuable solutions to their customers.

Over time, teams can eliminate a lot of this waiting by developing skills they need within the team. They often need manager help to do this, perhaps with permission to take training courses, connect to mentors, or build communities of practice. Managers generally have the connections and the organizational influence to help teams develop the skills and connections they need to become more self-sufficient.

ALIGNING SUPPORTING DEPARTMENTS

So far, we have focused on teams developing and delivering products and services used by customers, but most medium-sized and large organizations also have departments that support the rest of the organization with specialized skills, such as legal, human resources, and facilities management. What do these departments do?

First, the empowerment advantages we have discussed for teams that develop products and services are no less powerful for other teams. Decision latency lurks everywhere, so the people who are closest to the problem and with the greatest knowledge should make decisions about what they do and how they work.

Second, supporting departments should be staffed and organized so that teams producing products and services do not have to wait for specialized skills. This takes a couple of forms.

Sometimes, a product team needs specialized skills for days or even weeks while it works on some aspect of the product. For example, a team launching a new product often needs help with intellectual property law to make sure the assets of the organization are protected. Or it may need the expertise of information security professionals as it considers using third-party components or even as it develops its own components. For cases like this, the person or people with specialized skills may join the team temporarily to help resolve the issue.

When the need is smaller, like a consultation that can be concluded in a few hours, the best thing for the product team is for it to get the answers it needs without having to wait. Perhaps the team needs help finding job seekers as candidates for a new position, or it needs help working out an equitable team bonus-sharing plan. Sometimes, these questions can be scheduled for when a specialist is free, but in many cases, the team needs an answer immediately.

In most traditional organizations, specialists are highly paid and scarce, so product teams usually have to wait for the specialists to find space in their schedules. But it is expensive for a whole team of people to delay a decision because it cannot get the answers it needs.

In the case of specialists, *inverting the organization* means inverting the priorities so product teams never have to wait for help. This can be achieved using a combination of strategies:

- Hiring enough specialists to participate in the big-question work that can take days or weeks. These big questions do not unpredictably erupt out of nowhere; they are visible at least weeks in advance and are somewhat predictable.
- Having some people available "on demand" for shorter questions that take minutes or up to a few hours. Sometimes, these people do not require organizational knowledge and can be outsourced or filled with consultants who can be contracted to be available on demand.
- Gradually growing knowledge within teams for certain kinds of skills. Examples, include coaching team members on information security threats so they can do a better job themselves.
- Providing teams with self-service tools that replace the need for human help. Examples include portals where they can get answers to common questions about hiring and employment law or access to online hiring tools such as job boards.

Organizational Structure Is a Crutch

Many theories and models suggest how organizations can and should be structured. Some organizations choose to implement those theories and models slowly over time. Others take a faster big-bang "transformative" route. Both the slow-step or "transformation" strategies come with hopes and dreams of yielding dividends of new profits accompanied by happy customers and employees. However, we often see quite the opposite happen.

Organizational structures, from holacracy to corporate hierarchy, are a decision-making crutch for organizations. When things start going wrong, it is easy to blame the structure itself or blame the people for being unable to adapt to the structure.

We will not get into a philosophical debate over which models and structures we think are best. The reality is, in any given situation and moment, an organizational structure will work until it does not. What we would like to promote, regardless of your structure, is that the emphasis should be on people and their behaviors, not the structure itself. As we detailed in Chapter 1, your goals and what you measure drive the way people behave.

As organizations consider how their new structures will look, we often witness them freeze. All decision-making is halted, and anything new that should be considered is delayed until a new structure is put in place. That line of thinking is often antithetical to what they strive to do with their restructuring.

Ironically, it is never the organization's structure that leads to getting things done. Sometimes, it is in spite of it. Consider open-source projects, where anyone can contribute to the project according to how the community has decided to manage itself. Open-source has led to the most-used server operating system in the world, Linux, powerful development tools like the Eclipse Platform, and widely used server software like Apache, to name but a few. These kinds of open collaboration initiatives do not require huge organizations to get things done. They just need a clear mission, transparency, and people who are motivated by the mission to work together.

Some organizations think they need to devise the perfect organizational structure and put it in place before they can make changes. They know their organizational structure is part of the problem, and they want to fix it first to make subsequent changes easier. This is a mistake. Your organizational structure will never be perfect; in fact, no organizational structure is perfect. If you set goals and work toward them, adapting your organizational structure as you go along, you will get better, and your organization will adapt. All you need is a willingness to change anything that gets in the way of pursuing your goals over time.

SETTING AND ADAPTING GOALS

Throughout this book, we have talked about goals at three levels. Immediate tactical goals tend to be the domain of teams and can focus on any of the key value areas (CV, T2M, A2I, and UV). Because of their short-term nature, they tend to focus on short-term improvements and immediate benefits.

Intermediate goals focus on products and their associated CV or UV. Intermediate goals provide a longer-term target for teams but also indicate to leaders that the organization is moving in the right direction toward strategic goals.

Strategic goals are closely tied to the mission of the organization. Because intermediate goals are more effective targets, strategic goals tend to be informative and inspirational. Because they are also largely *aspirational*, are mostly used to inform shorter-term goals.

Although everyone in the organization contributes to achieving goals, all have a stake in them and participate, at least to some degree, in their creation. Strategic goals, however, are most closely associated with senior leadership because they help establish norms and targets for the organization.

MOST GOALS CAN—AND SHOULD—CHANGE

Because they are focused on a short timespan, immediate tactical goals generally take a few weeks and do not change. All other goals can change—and should—when the organization obtains new information that helps them see that the goal, as stated, is a little (or sometimes a lot) off.

Organizations may find that market conditions have changed. They may find that customer preferences have changed. They may also find that the assumptions that shaped their goal creation were incorrect. Whatever the reason, goals can and should change based on feedback—not because teams or the organization cannot meet them but because they will lead the organization in the wrong direction.

In a complex world, even goals are forever shifting. For that reason, organizations should not invest a lot in crafting perfect goals. If you are using feedback and continuously adapting and refining your goals, they will get better as you work.

Some organizations spend a lot of time and money trying to manage the facts to fit their predetermined narratives of success. This only renders organizations unable to learn. To escape this trap, they have to be willing to embrace the unexpected.

WHAT TO WATCH FOR

Some leaders tend to use measurement as a simplistic carrot-and-stick tool. They want to find measures they can use to reward people for producing good results and punish them for producing bad results. They want a common dashboard for the organization that will easily identify the teams they consider high performers and figure out what those high-performing teams are doing differently from the perceived low performers. Then, they want to make all teams do what the high performers do.

This is, at best, superficial and, at worst, deeply harmful. There are no best practices. You cannot copy good performance from one team and copy-paste it onto others. Every team is dealing with different challenges and has to find its own way to succeed. Measurement helps these teams clearly see where they are and what they need to improve to reach their goals. When measurement becomes a motivational or punishment tool, people focus their efforts on embellishing their accomplishments and hiding their failures. In doing so, they destroy transparency and render measurement meaningless.

Never treat a dashboard as facts in stone. Metrics are just starting points for conversations. When coupled with goals, they help organizations and their teams steer toward worthwhile and ambitious goals. Along the path toward those goals, they help teams talk about how they can improve and what help they need to achieve those goals. When organizations tie metrics to rewards and punishments, they stop these conversations and can use the metrics to improve.

False security is the other thing to watch out for. We are not sure if it is human nature or a learned response, but people tend to believe others who speak with conviction and certainty. They sound convincing, so what they say must be true. We think open and transparent conversations about data are more valuable and productive, even when they expose uncomfortable truths.

Leaders must create the space for others to embrace transparency, and they need to embrace it themselves. Leaders in traditional organizations are often expected to have all the answers. It takes courage and humility to say, "I do not know, but let me find out." It also takes courage and patience to confront new data that does not conform to expectations.

MOVING FORWARD

We started this book by talking about setting goals and using evidence obtained by experimentation to seek toward those goals. This may seem daunting, but evidence-based management asks only that you experiment, measure, and learn to improve toward your goals.

In many organizations, planning is paramount. Teams are expected to perform to plans or even exceed them. When they do not, they are criticized. No one seems to question the plan, but they should. A plan is simply a set of guesses about how things should happen to achieve a result, but plans can be wrong. You need plans to help people collaborate to reach a goal, but you also need to adapt those plans to incorporate what you learn along the way, both about the goal and the path you need to take toward the goal. The more uncertain your path, the more you must adapt it as you learn.

To avoid wasting effort, your plans should be as short in scope as possible—no longer than a few weeks. With your goals in mind, you only need to plan for the next step. As you take that step, you gather data, or evidence, to help you decide what to do after that. All the while, you ask yourself, "Are we getting closer to our goal?"

But where should you start? Trying to change your entire organization immediately is a sure path to disappointment. Try something smaller—a single product or service—something a team or a small number of teams can deliver. To get started, you might need to carve off a simpler product, as we discussed in Chapter 6, "Applying EBM at the Product Level." And you might need to simplify your team's collaboration by bringing all the necessary skills into a single team, as we noted earlier in this chapter.

You will probably need to reframe or even re-create the strategic goal(s) for this product or service. You will need to look at why customers buy it. What unmet outcomes are they trying to achieve? From there, you need to look at the KVAs we mentioned in Chapter 1 for hints on what things you might need to improve as you set intermediate and immediate tactical goals. And then it is just a matter of continually framing experiments for improvement, running those experiments, and adapting your next steps (your next experiments.)

We started with helping teams become more effective (Chapter 3) because most teams need to work on their ability to deliver before they can be effective at running experiments about customer value. And Chapter 4, "Managing and Overcoming Expectations," and Chapter 5, "Separating the Signal from the Noise," will give you some ideas about how to overcome past inertia to try working in a new way.

Once you have embraced empiricism and managed a few products guided by these new insights, you will want to try looking across products to make better choices about where you spend your time and energy. Chapter 7, "Applying EBM at the Portfolio Level," provides some ideas to try and techniques to master. By the time you are working on improving your abilities to manage a portfolio of products and services, you will also need to work on improving your organization.

We cannot say where this will take you, but our experience tells us that if you embrace experimentation and empiricism, as we have outlined in this book, you will progress toward your goals in ways you have not experienced before.

INDEX